IF NOT NOW THEN WHEN

"Few people understand Canada's pulse like Faytene Grasseschi. This book is both a wake-up call and a roadmap for true impact."

—The Hon. Stockwell Day

Former Leader of the Official Opposition, Parliament of Canada

"We can all learn from Faytene's passion for building a stronger Canada through meaningful civic engagement. As CTZNs, we share both the privilege and the responsibility to engage in the political life of our nation. Pericles once warned, 'Just because you do not take an interest in politics doesn't mean politics won't take an interest in you.' This book is an essential read for anyone who wants to understand what's truly at stake, and to discover what they can do right now to help shape Canada's future."

—David Craig

Host of CTZN - Director / MCA Media Group

"Brilliantly presented in coffee-shop language, Faytene's book *If Not Now Then When* is engaging, direct, and compelling! Her present-day examples of close wins and close losses remind the reader that 'just showing up' can change the trajectory of an entire nation. Now it's time to get off the couch!"

—Dr. Phil Nordin

Chairman, CONNECT Leaders Group

"Faytene's book is a wake-up call for anyone who loves Canada, and believes their voice still matters. It's bold, hopeful, and reminds us that faith and courage in everyday life can truly shape a nation's future."

—Jeremy Prest

Co-Host, The Citizen Podcast

"What you are about to read is one of the most compelling and thought-provoking books of this season, addressing the unique challenges within our Canadian context and culture. We are living in a window of opportunity—a moment pregnant with purpose and destiny—that will help determine the future course of our nation.

Faytene Grasseschi has skillfully woven together a powerful message, drawing from history, current data, and personal experience. She issues a clear call for faith-filled Canadians to engage now if we want to preserve the freedoms shaped by our biblical, Judeo-Christian values—values that have helped make Canada one of the most desirable democracies in the world.

I encourage you to share this book widely—for the sake of our families, our children, and future generations."

—Giulio Lorefice Gabeli

National Director, Canada Celebrates Israel (CCI) Network of Jews & Christians

"Drawing on decades of persistent political advocacy, Faytene offers readers deeply personal, and passionate insights in this compelling book. Her message about the need for hopeful, and tenacious civic engagement is a clarion call to Canadians across the country. This book offers a thoughtful, and practical guide for those who want to make a difference in Canada in this crucial historical moment."

—Lia Milousis

Human Rights Lawyer, Author of
"An Inconvenient Life"

IF NOT NOW THEN WHEN

WHY THIS MOMENT MATTERS FOR CANADA AND WHAT WE CAN DO ABOUT IT

FAYTENE GRASSESCHI

FIRST PRINT EDITION | IF NOT NOW THEN WHEN © FAYTENE GRASSESCHI

01 25

LIBRARY AND ARCHIVES CANADA

ISBN 978-1-998412-42-6 (paperback)

Printed in Canada

FiveArrowsMedia
FIVEARROWSMEDIA.COM

DEDICATION

To my children, whom I love with all my heart and will fight for with all my might, you are one of our primary motivations.

To my husband, thank you for your heroic support and love.

To our parents, thank you for showing us how to live for the next generation. We honour you.

To all those who show up when it matters, thank you. Much respect.

Desiderantes Meliorem Patriam

"...THEY WERE LONGING FOR A BETTER COUNTRY..."

HEBREWS 11:16

MOTTO OF THE ORDER OF CANADA[1]

PREFACE

There are moments in life when you can almost feel history leaning forward—waiting to see what we will do. I believe we are living in one of those moments right now.

When I began writing *If Not Now Then When*, I didn't do so as a politician or academic, but as a mother, a Canadian, and a person who loves this nation deeply. Like many of you, I have watched our freedoms erode, our economy falter, and our culture drift from the values that once anchored us.[1] I have felt the same ache and urgency that so many others feel—the sense that something must change, and soon.

This book was born from that place. It is a call to courage and clarity in a time of confusion. It is also a reminder that ordinary citizens—not elites, not institutions—have always been the ones who steer nations back toward truth and freedom. Every effort, every conversation, and every act of service and civic engagement matters more than most realize.

When I look at the Canada that my children are growing up in, I am both burdened and hopeful. Burdened, because the stakes are real—freedom of speech, of conscience, and of life itself are being tested in ways few of us imagined possible. Hopeful, because I know the heart of the Canadian people: we are principled, courageous, and capable of being great agents for change when awakened.[2]

As you read these pages, my hope and prayer are that you will feel both informed and inspired—that you will see the challenges clearly but also sense the invitation to stand with conviction in this moment. To whom much is given, much is required. We have inherited a nation built on courage, compassion, and faith; now it is our turn to steward it well.

This book is not meant to condemn, but to awaken. It is not about politics alone, but about legacy—the kind we will leave to our children and grandchildren. My desire is that every reader, regardless of background, will come away with a renewed sense of agency and hope. We cannot change everything, but we can change something—and when enough of us do, the course of a nation can shift.

If you love Canada, if you care about truth and freedom, and if you believe that faith, hope, and love still have a role to play in public life—then you are part of the answer. This is our time to rise with courage, to speak with grace, and to act with purpose.

The challenges before us are great, but the potential for renewal is greater still. The story of Canada is not finished. The next chapter belongs to those who show up.

If not us, who?

If not now, then when?

With hope,

Faytene Grasseschi

TABLE OF CONTENTS

Foreword by Doug Sharpe 1

CHAPTER 1
Could This Be Our Turning Point? 5

CHAPTER 2
Lessons from Distant and
Not So Distant History 21

CHAPTER 3
Stewarding the Economy 37

CHAPTER 4
Protecting Freedom 53

CHAPTER 5
The Value of Life 69

CHAPTER 6
Culture at the Crossroads 83

CHAPTER 7
Build Smart, Build Together 99

CHAPTER 8
A Practical Road Map and
the Most Important Action 111

CHAPTER 9
The Nation Goes to
Those Who Show Up 137

Conclusion 145

Acknowledgements 151

Recommended Reading 153

Endnotes 155

About the Author 173

FOREWORD

Faytene's message in *If Not Now Then When* is both timely and urgent.

As Canadians of faith, we are being called to awaken, to act, and to steward this nation according to principles that protect families, defend freedom, safeguard the vulnerable, and ensure a just inheritance for our children.

The four pillars that guide our own work at Canada Family Action—parental authority, freedom of belief, protection of the vulnerable, and fiscal responsibility—resonate deeply throughout these pages.

This book reminds us that our nation's future depends not on governments alone, but on citizens who will courageously stand, speak, and show up—for Canada, for truth, and for hope.

I encourage all citizens to commit to supporting the work we can, and must, do together on the road ahead. The Canada we leave to our children will benefit greatly from our efforts.

—Doug Sharpe

President, Canada Family Action
Host, National Leadership Briefing

COURAGE IS THE FIRST OF HUMAN QUALITIES BECAUSE IT IS THE QUALITY WHICH GUARANTEES ALL THE OTHERS.

—WINSTON CHURCHILL

CHAPTER 1

COULD THIS BE OUR TURNING POINT?

Every generation has moments that shake it awake, hinges of history where everything turns. For many, the recent assassination of Charlie Kirk was such a moment.

Kirk's murder stopped people in their tracks and reminded us all of something we'd quietly known but perhaps not admitted: voices who courageously defend the freedoms we take for granted, and the future we hope to secure for our children, are more critical and endangered than we realized.

Charlie was more than a political and cultural commentator. He was a father, a husband, a leader, and a man of unwavering conviction and faith. He was a constant and steady presence in the public square, unafraid to speak when others stayed silent, unafraid to engage when others withdrew.

But what truly made him unique in our time was his belief that we owed one another the dignity of honest dialogue. Even if he did not agree with someone, he would defend their right to hold and express their views while seeking to authentically lay out the logic behind his own. Particularly in his latter years of public debate on college campuses, he could be observed leaning towards those who challenged him ideologically, modelling kindness, civility, and genuine compassion. In this way, even if a person disagreed with his stance on an issue (and many did), it was hard not to respect his commitment to engage in dialogue. He would often state, *"As soon as we stop talking, everyone loses."* He was right.

This is precisely why, when a fatal bullet penetrated his neck before an entire generation, in broad daylight on a college campus—the very place where free ideas should be debated, not silenced—the world shuddered.

His death was more than the end of a man, father, husband, and leader's life. His murder was a direct hit on freedom and a mass act of intimidation for those with similar views.

In the hours, days, and weeks following those who held to faith, family, and freedom principles worldwide were confronted with the harsh reality that these views could be fatal. The logical thought progression: will we choose fear and self-censorship, or courage?

A TURNING POINT FOR CANADIANS

The truth is that, for generations, we Canadians have assumed we would always have freedom. Now, whether considering Charlie's assassination,

> *The truth is that, for generations, we Canadians have assumed we would always have freedom.*

the freezing of the bank account of a single mom in British Columbia for donating to the Trucker's Convoy, a variety of professionals across Canada losing their jobs for not breaching their medical conscience or the very recent flurry of federal bills being tabled in Parliament—which if passed could expand hate speech legislation and give the government power to cut the phone lines and internet connections of those they deem to be a threat.[1] The bottom line is this: the freedoms so many have felt would always be here are being tested.

So again, the question is simple: will we be silenced, or will we draw a courageous line in the sand and continue to walk with heads held high to the front lines of social engagement to shape a better tomorrow for our kids and theirs?

RESPECT WITHOUT APOLOGY

Too often, conservative-minded Canadians—young and old—have been told that if we express our convictions, we are being hateful or divisive. Any genuine observer knows this is blatantly false.

There are hateful people on all sides of the political and ideological spectrum. There are also loving and kind people on all sides of the spectrum, and at all points in between! The issue is not a person's ideology; it is their conduct. I experienced this firsthand as a political candidate when a man put his two large German Shepherd dogs on a charge in my direction while canvassing. I was denied service at a hair salon, screamed at in public, told to kill myself, and lied about on social media—all because I was the local conservative candidate, and possibly because of my Christian faith. The face of hate can show up anywhere. It is not partisan.

The reality is that if someone can label another for their views, they can justify not listening to them. As free-thinking Canadians, we must resist this behaviour and be bigger—speaking what we believe with courage while genuinely taking time to hear those who disagree with us. Each person has value. In the end, we may still disagree, but we can be civil.

We must also recognize and reinforce, through courage, the truth that free societies depend on open debate, on hearing competing ideas, and on citizens willing to wrestle with differences. Strong values do not weaken democracy—they strengthen it. This is where we must also address a point that some shy away from: the values that built the free societies we now enjoy were largely shaped by biblical principles.

The idea of loving your neighbour as yourself, the belief that every human being carries inherent worth, the conviction that families are the foundation of society, and the practice of enterprise, honest work, and spending within your means—these have been the backbone of flourishing nations. Far from being something to hide, these values need to be trumpeted and celebrated. They are the reason Canada, and the West in general, became prosperous and free.

To be clear: you don't have to be a Christian to cherish these values. But we should all acknowledge that they are part of our inheritance, and we abandon them at our peril.

THE COST OF SILENCE

The temptation for many Canadians—especially people of faith—is to stay private. To keep opinions to ourselves. To focus on our own families and communities, and leave "politics" to others. But history tells us that when good people withdraw, the results are rarely good.

The flourishing of our society has always depended on citizens willing to step into the public square with courage and respect. Sometimes they have been politicians. More often, they have been ordinary people who simply refused to stay silent when it mattered.

When those who hold to time-tested values withdraw from public life, the only voices left are often those driving agendas that undermine family, weaken freedom, and destabilize society.

Silence is not safety. It is surrender. If we do not show up, if we do not speak and engage, then decisions will still be made—just not for the benefit of future generations.

THE CONSEQUENCES OF FORGETTING

History also warns us what happens when societies forget their roots. Nations that devalue human life, silence dissent, or weaken the family eventually decline. Rome collapsed not just from outside invasion but from internal decay.[2] Authoritarian governments gain ground when the population shrinks back from defending their values.

Canada is not immune. Our freedoms are not self-sustaining. They depend on us showing up, generation after generation, to defend and reinforce them. If we forget, we lose.

CANADA'S MOMENT OF DECISION

I believe our nation is in a critical window, and that if we don't begin to turn things around, and fast, the Canada that we have all known and loved may soon be a distant memory. If you are reading this, I believe you may share this concern. Thank you for your love, care, and engagement with me in these pages. I do not take it lightly.

Freedom of expression is under strain. Our economy is weighed down by debt, driving up inflation and taxation.[3] Life itself, from its beginning to its natural end, is being devalued. And yet, while some may feel despondent and powerless, the reality is that in election after election, the outcomes have often been decided by razor-thin margins—sometimes just a few hundred votes, sometimes fewer. The masses have not determined our current trajectory. Rather, as you will see through the examples in this book, it is a small group of engaged Canadians who have gotten involved over the last decades who have created the Canada we know today. They are not the elites; they are the engaged.

That means ordinary Canadians, people like you and me, hold extraordinary power. Every conversation matters. Every volunteer matters. Every vote matters. The difference between decline and renewal may come down to whether we decide to step forward or sit back. It may feel daunting, even overwhelming. But history shows us that determined, intelligent, and organized minorities have often shaped the destiny of nations. It will be no different for our future.

COURAGE FOR TODAY

Here is the question: when future generations look back on this moment, what will they see? Will they see mothers and fathers who gave up, too afraid to defend what is good and true, intimidated by bullets in the public square? Or will they see mothers and fathers who rose to the challenge, who recognized that the freedoms and prosperity we enjoy did not come cheaply, and that they are not guaranteed for our kids unless we stand for them today?

On the day Charlie Kirk was murdered, I remember distinctly thinking, "This. Is. A. Turning. Point." It was, and it must be.

The assassination of Charlie Kirk is a tragedy. But if it awakens us—if it calls us to step forward, to speak with courage and respect, and to defend the values that make societies flourish—then it can also be the beginning of renewal.

The choice is ours. If not now, then when?

TAKE 5

1. **Freedom is fragile.** Charlie's assassination was a wake-up call—a reminder that freedom is never guaranteed. If we don't defend it with courage, we will lose it.

---

2. **Courage with civility.** Charlie showed that conviction and compassion can coexist. We must speak truth boldly while treating others with respect and grace.

---

3. **Silence is surrender.** Withdrawing from the public square doesn't protect us—it concedes it. We must show up, speak up, and stand firm for faith, family, and freedom.

---

4. **Freedom has roots.** Our liberty was built on biblical principles—human dignity, family, honesty, and love for neighbour. Forgetting these values leads to decline.

---

5. Ordinary Canadians matter. Our nation's future will be shaped not by elites but by engaged citizens. Every vote, every act of courage, every voice counts.

A SMALL GROUP OF THOUGHTFUL, COMMITTED CITIZENS CAN CHANGE THE WORLD; INDEED, IT'S THE ONLY THING THAT EVER HAS.

— MARGARET MEAD

CHAPTER 2

LESSONS FROM DISTANT AND NOT SO DISTANT HISTORY

When we look at the challenges before Canada today, it's easy to feel like the problems are too big, the forces against us too powerful. But history tells a different story. Time and again, small groups of determined people have shaped the future. They didn't wait for the perfect moment or for overwhelming support. They acted when it mattered. They discerned the times; they knew what to do and did not grow weary in well-doing. As a result, they saw change.

This chapter is about remembering lessons from Canada's distant and not-so-distant past, and from the broader world, that prove this to be true.

THE POWER OF THE FEW

Our Confederation was not inevitable. It was the vision of a small circle of leaders—Macdonald, Cartier, Brown, and a handful of others—who pushed through fierce opposition to create a nation out of scattered colonies. At the time, many thought it was impossible. Yet because they refused to give up, Canada was born.

In Britain, William Wilberforce and a small group of allies spent decades fighting the slave trade. Wilberforce's core group—often referred to as the Clapham Sect—was composed of roughly a dozen key members, with a broader network of around 20-30 regular collaborators over time.[1] This small group was mocked, ignored, and opposed. Yet their persistence eventually led to the abolition of the slave trade—changing the moral course of a nation and influencing the world. In the United States, Martin Luther

King Jr. and the civil rights movement began as a relatively small band of committed leaders and citizens who insisted on dignity and equality.[2] They faced violent opposition, but their determination reshaped law and culture.

The lesson of history is simply this: you don't need everyone to act. You just need enough people to act at the right time.

SMALL NUMBERS, BIG CHANGE

An example from our own national history is the 1995 Quebec referendum.[3] Voter turnout was exceptionally high at 93.52%, with more than 4 million people voting. The official results were: "Yes" (for sovereignty): 49.42%—2,308,360 votes and "No" (against sovereignty): 50.58%—2,362,648 votes. The "No" side won by a margin of only 54,288 votes. This referendum was one of the closest referendums in Canadian history, with a margin of barely over 1%.

We like to think democracy turns on sweeping movements and tidal waves of opinion. In truth, it often turns on inches—on who showed up, who didn't, and who cared enough to get involved.

Recent examples in Canada are equally dramatic.

THE MYTH OF IRRELEVANCE

Many Canadians have quietly adopted a myth: *my one vote doesn't matter.* The evidence says otherwise.

- In the **2025 federal election**, several swing ridings were decided by margins in the low hundreds.[4] In Terrebonne (Quebec), one vote would have made a difference.[5] After all the recounts were completed, Mark Carney missed forming a majority government by only 57 votes spread across three very tight races: Windsor–Tecumseh–Lakeshore (4 vote difference), Terra Nova–The Peninsulas (12 vote difference), and Nunavut (41 vote difference).[6]
- In **October of 2025**, the mayoral race in Calgary was decided by fewer than 500 votes out of almost 350,000 cast, less than 0.15%. This is one medium-sized church.[7]

In the same municipal election, a strong faith, family, and freedom candidate won Mayor of Beaumont by approximately 200 votes, or one volunteer.[8]

- In New Brunswick's **2024 provincial election**, my own race was decided by 224 votes out of 8,291 votes cast.[9] One more volunteer, one more carpool, one more family talking to friends, getting out to vote, and I would be an elected official today.
- In that same election (**2024**), Premier Blaine Higgs's seat was lost by 183 votes; again, one volunteer would have changed that outcome.[10]
- In **2023**, Premier Danielle Smith won a majority government by 5 seats. The tightest race was won by 129 votes. Adding the difference in the five closest races, she won her majority by a little more than 2,000 votes (Calgary-North, won by 129, Calgary-North West, won by 143, Calgary-Cross, won by 514, Calgary-Bow,

won by 623, and Lethbridge-East, won by 636).[11]

- In **2019**, the federal election produced a minority Liberal government. The combined difference between victory and defeat across just a few dozen ridings was fewer than 25,000 votes—roughly the population of a small municipality.[12]

- A friend of mine lost her federal nomination by 12 votes—the number of people you can fit around a kitchen table. Many of her supporters were certain she would win and chose to attend a church conference rather than go to vote on the day of the nomination. Because they did not show, she lost. Had she won, she likely would have been a Member of Parliament for several decades because of the conservative support in that riding.

- **In 2013**, Justin Trudeau became leader of the Liberal Party because just over 81,000 Canadians joined the Liberal Party and voted for him.[13] Mathematically, this means

> that only 0.23% of Canadians determined the leader of the Liberal Party of Canada that year, and set him on his trajectory to becoming the next Prime Minister.

I could go on for pages with examples that all illustrate the same point: our political future is determined not by the majority of voices, but by the minority who show up.

Presence is powerful, but so is absence.

WHY ENGAGEMENT MATTERS

> *The question is never whether our nation will be shaped, but by whom.*

Voter turnout in Canada hovers around 60% for federal elections, 45-60% for provincial elections, and much lower for municipal elections.[14] In other words, four out of ten eligible Canadians regularly give their voice to someone else.

Politics shapes everything from taxes to education to how freely you can speak or worship. When people disengage, decisions don't disappear—they're simply made by others. The question is never *whether* our nation will be shaped, but *by whom*.

Democracy works best when citizens participate early and consistently, not sporadically. Showing up only when angered by an issue is like checking your smoke alarm after the fire has started.

THE TIPPING POINT OF VOLUNTEERS

Elections are not won by slogans alone; they are won by people. Every campaign manager can tell you that a single committed volunteer who makes phone calls or knocks on doors is worth dozens of votes each and every shift. Multiply that by a few hundred volunteers, and consistent engagement over a 4–6 week campaign, and you shift entire ridings.

A POWERFUL ILLUSTRATION

During the 2025 federal election, 4 My Canada, in partnership with another non-profit, dispatched more than 1,300 volunteers to 75 high-quality candidate campaigns.[15] Forty-six of those candidates won. Statistical modelling showed a probability that those efforts likely changed the outcome in three to ten ridings—the difference between a majority and a minority Liberal government.

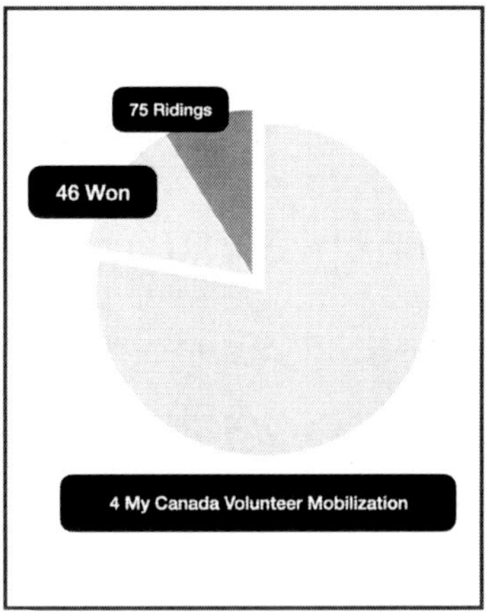

Had the Liberals received a majority, several of their bills would already be in the Senate receiving royal assent. Because they were held to a minority, opposition parties now have the opportunity to analyze bills critically, bring amendments at committee or vote against them with the possibility of defeating them.

Numbers don't lie. Organized citizens change outcomes.

Think of democracy like a balance scale. Most of the weight is already evenly distributed—party loyalty, habit, and regional identity. But at the tipping point, one small weight can shift everything. That weight might be your vote, your phone call, a bit of your time volunteering, or your encouragement to a neighbour.

Canada's system is built for participation. Unlike some countries where power is centralized, ours responds quickly to small changes. This is a gift—and a responsibility.

FAITH AND CONVICTION IN THE PUBLIC SQUARE

The same values that make good neighbours—honesty, service, stewardship—make good citizens.

The early abolitionists, reformers, and builders of Canada were people whose moral compass came from faith. They didn't withdraw; they acted. We can do the same today and make a real impact, and we must never forget that freedom survives when people of conviction bring their values into the open, not when they hide them under fear of criticism.

One of the most effective ways to make an impact is to focus energy where it matters most—

swing ridings, leadership races, nominations, and local councils. National headlines often start with small, targeted actions at the local level.

Other communities have learned this well. Across Canada, and in every election, ethnic groups, professional associations, and advocacy networks mobilize strategically to elect leaders who reflect their priorities. There is nothing wrong with that; it's how democracy functions. Christians and value-based citizens can, and should, do the same—thoughtfully, lawfully, and respectfully.

A SHARED TRUST AND RESPONSIBILITY

Civic engagement is both a right and a duty. Generations before us fought, served, and sacrificed so that every citizen could have a voice. Choosing not to vote or engage is not neutrality—it is forfeiture.

Elections are often decided by the number of people you can fit in a single church, gym, or community hall. The difference between a nation moving toward renewal or decline may be the handful who believed their participation mattered.

In the next few chapters, we will take a deeper look at some of our nation's greatest crisis points and give some concise and simple action points that can be taken to really make a difference.

TAKE 5

1. History proves small groups change nations. From the Fathers of Confederation to Wilberforce and Martin Luther King Jr., decisive moments have always been shaped by a few who discerned the times and acted with courage, not by crowds waiting for permission.

---

2. Big outcomes hinge on small margins. Elections and referendums are often decided by handfuls of votes—sometimes by the size of a church congregation. Presence is powerful, but so is absence.

---

3. Engagement—not numbers—creates impact. Democracy responds to those who participate. A single volunteer, one family, or one ballot can shift the balance of power. Organized citizens shape outcomes.

---

4. Faith and conviction belong in the public square. The same biblical principles that built Canada—honesty, service, stewardship—still strengthen it today. Freedom endures when people of faith bring their values into the open, not when they hide them.

---

5. Civic duty is a sacred trust. Generations before us fought for the right to vote and speak freely. Choosing not to engage isn't neutrality—it's surrender. The future of our nation depends on those willing to believe their participation matters.

YOU CAN'T
SPEND
YOUR WAY INTO
PROSPERITY.

— MARGARET THATCHER

CHAPTER 3

STEWARDING THE ECONOMY

When a household spends more than it earns, everyone knows what happens: sooner or later, the bills come due. The same is true for nations.

Yet in recent decades, Canada—like much of the Western world—has slipped into the habit of borrowing from tomorrow to pay for today. Each new budget brings promises, programs, and deficits that quietly pile up on the shoulders of our children and grandchildren.

THE BURDEN OF DEBT

Canada's federal debt has now surpassed the trillion-dollar mark. That means every man, woman, and child born today in Canada has tens of thousands of dollars in public debt that they didn't personally choose.

As of the fall of 2025, the Canadian Taxpayers' Federation website noted that each Canadian's personal federal debt portion is more than $30,000 and that the federal debt is growing by more than $100 million a day.[1]

If you live in Newfoundland and Labrador, Quebec, or Ontario, you can add an estimated $30,000 to the provincial debt per capita, meaning Canadians in these provinces have a personal debt burden of almost $60,000 per person.[2] For a family of four, that is almost a quarter of a million dollars!

Every other province is somewhere in the $14,000–$27,000 range, meaning that even the least indebted Canadians have an estimated

$44,000 in public debt, with the federal and provincial portions combined.

What does this mean practically? Plainly put, it means more of our hard-earned money is going to pay interest on federal or provincial debts rather than being spent on critical infrastructure and services such as building hospitals, schools, seniors' care centres, repairing roads and bridges, or supporting innovation.[3]

In the 2024-2025 fiscal year, it is estimated that Canadians will pay more than $50 billion in interest on the federal debt, approximately $137 million per day. The waste is colossal.[4]

It's easy to think of debt as abstract, but it is not. It shows up in higher taxes, fewer services, slower growth, and reduced freedom to act when a crisis comes. Every dollar spent on interest is a dollar not spent building the future.

In September of 2025, assessing Canada's financial situation, the Parliamentary Budget Officer, Interim Jason Jacques, said this:

> "It's not a funny fiscal outlook… it's a really serious fiscal outlook. We don't lightly use the word 'unsustainable.' Unsustainable means you don't have the option of saying, 'Maybe I'll wait a couple of years, I'll see how things go.' It means if you don't change, this is done. Right? So…it's very serious."[5]

Our parents and grandparents built this country by saving, investing, and planning for the next generation. Today, we are trending in the opposite direction—spending what future Canadians have yet to earn.

As interest costs consume an ever-growing share of our national resources, the question becomes not whether we can afford to act, but whether we can afford not to. True stewardship demands courage and discipline today so that future generations can inherit freedom, not debt.

A QUESTION OF STEWARDSHIP

Managing a nation's finances is not only an economic issue; it's a question of stewardship and even morality. Whether you view it through a biblical lens or simply common sense, the principle is the same: we are caretakers of what we've been given.

For those who draw on Scripture, Proverbs 22:7 warns that *"...the borrower is servant to the lender,"* and Proverbs 13:22 teaches, *"A good man leaves an inheritance to his children's children..."* (KJV).[6] It is both unwise and immoral to pass debt onto future generations, enslaving them to our lenders rather than giving them the opportunity to build for their children. But even apart from faith, experience confirms it—debt limits freedom. It binds governments and citizens alike to decisions made long ago.

Good stewardship means taking responsibility, living within our means, and thinking beyond the next election cycle. It means leaders making hard choices instead of popular ones, and citizens holding them accountable for it.

THE EXAMPLE OF SOUND MANAGEMENT

The good news is that some leaders have shown that this can be done.

Premier Blaine Higgs was elected in 2018, inheriting a province in fiscal crisis. In 2019, the Canadian Tax Journal published an article asking the question, "*Is New Brunswick Heading over the Fiscal Cliff?*"[7] Through wise and prudent management, Premier Higgs turned the province around. Government net debt fell from approximately $23,657 per person (at the start of the combined period under Premier Higgs & his predecessor) to about $14,287 per person.[8]

His management earned him the Fraser Institute's distinction as the best fiscal manager of a province for multiple years.[9] He maintained fiscal discipline, and the province's finances remained stable for five consecutive years. Under his watch, credit ratings improved, and future generations were given breathing room.

In 2024, he lost the election to Susan Holt and the Liberals. Tragically, his fiscal record was quickly reversed. The province slid back toward deficit spending. It was a stark reminder that economic stewardship is fragile—it depends on people willing to protect it and voters willing to vote for it.

...economic stewardship is fragile—it depends on people willing to protect it and voters willing to vote for it.

On the federal level, in the 1990s, a Liberal government—under pressure from citizens demanding change—took bold action to balance the books. Within a few years, Canada went from near-crisis to surplus. It can be done again, but only if the public insists on it.

FREEDOM AND THE MARKETPLACE

Furthermore, a healthy economy is about more than government budgets. It is also about protecting the freedom to create, build, and take risks. Free enterprise—ordinary people starting small businesses, inventing, hiring, and investing—has lifted more people out of poverty than any government program in history.

This spirit of entrepreneurship has deep roots in our national story.[10] Settlers and immigrants built Canada through hard work and innovation. Family farms, corner stores, trades, and small enterprises have been the backbone of our communities for generations. When governments over-tax, over-regulate, or discourage initiative, that backbone weakens.

Economic stewardship, therefore, isn't only about balancing spreadsheets; it's about defending the freedom that allows individuals and families to prosper.

THE MORAL DIMENSION

Whether we talk about national budgets or personal finances, the principle is simple: we should not consume what belongs to our children. A nation that spends recklessly today and sends the bill to tomorrow is betraying its own future. We are responsible for leaving our nation stronger, not weaker—to hand our children opportunity, not obligation.

Debt, when it becomes a lifestyle, undermines more than credit ratings. It erodes character. It teaches short-term thinking instead of long-term building. It conditions citizens to expect benefits without sacrifice. And once that mindset sets in, it's hard to reverse.

THE STAKES FOR THE NEXT GENERATION

Imagine a young couple today, working hard, raising kids, trying to buy a home, facing record high housing prices, and taxes that rise faster than wages. Now imagine them doing it in a country where public debt keeps growing and inflation erodes every dollar they earn. That is not sustainable.

We owe it to them to course-correct. Our children should inherit a nation that rewards effort, protects opportunity, and uses resources wisely—not one drowning in obligations they never agreed to.

Now also imagine a senior who has worked hard their entire life, paid their bills, saved, invested, paid their taxes, and done all the right things. They have done what they needed to sustain themselves in their final years but there is a problem—prices keep going up and up and up. Eventually, it becomes clear that what they have saved is not sufficient to keep the heat and lights on and food in the fridge..

Having faithfully paid taxes their entire life—and knowing that they can't make ends meet, they look to the government that they have given their hard-earned income to for decades. However, because of massive debt spending and hundreds of millions in weekly interest payments, there is nothing left to give back to the people.

Instead of offering provision as a repayment for decades of tax investment, the government says, "I am so sorry, but I can't offer you help to pay the bills, but if life is too hard to handle now, we can help you end your life through medical assistance in dying. Would you like that?"

This scenario is chilling. What is even more chilling is that it is not dystopian. Stories of senior veterans and disabled Canadians being offered state-administered suicide rather than the assistance they are seeking have hit national headlines.[11] The reality is this: when economies bottom out, it can lead to gross social injustice.

Economic stewardship may not be the most glamorous issue, but it is one of the most important. It determines whether we have the freedom to act when a crisis comes, the strength to invest in our future, and the integrity to keep our word to those who need us today.

Let us remember: a jurisdiction that learns to live within its means will thrive; a nation that forgets this simple truth will slowly lose the freedom it once enjoyed.

The good news is that decline is not destiny, and with restraint, innovation, resource development, and resolve, we can turn it around.

As already mentioned, this starts with citizens understanding the issue, discussing it openly, and voting for leaders willing to make disciplined choices. It also starts with each of us practicing the same principle at home: save more, waste less, and live within our means. A culture of responsibility at the kitchen table becomes a culture of responsibility in Parliament.

The next chapter turns to another cornerstone of a healthy country—protecting freedom itself. For without freedom, even the strongest economy cannot stand for long. As a result, they saw change.

TAKE 5

1. Debt is not abstract—it's personal. Every dollar the government borrows today becomes a burden on our children tomorrow. Each family already carries tens of thousands in public debt they never chose.

---

2. Stewardship is moral, not just fiscal. Managing national finances is a question of right and wrong. Scripture and common sense both teach that we are to live within our means and leave an inheritance, not a liability.

---

3. Discipline works—and its absence costs us. Provinces like New Brunswick proved that responsible management restores stability. But when voters reward short-term spending, progress unravels almost overnight.

---

4. Free enterprise is freedom in action. A strong economy depends on individuals free to create, build, and innovate. When over-taxation or regulation crush initiative, the nation weakens at its core.

---

5. Responsibility begins at home. Fiscal renewal starts with citizens choosing to save, plan, and live wisely. A culture of stewardship in our households becomes the foundation for stewardship in Parliament.

THE PRICE OF FREEDOM IS ETERNAL VIGILANCE.

— THOMAS JEFFERSON

CHAPTER 4

PROTECTING FREEDOM

Freedom is like air. You rarely think about it until it's gone. Yet across the world—and increasingly in Canada—freedom is being tested, restricted, and in some cases quietly redefined.

For generations, Canadians assumed that our freedoms were secure: freedom of speech, of belief, of conscience, of parental authority, and of peaceful assembly. This is in part due to the fact that it is outlined in Section 2 of the Canadian Charter of Rights and Freedoms, which states,

> **Everyone has the following fundamental freedoms:**
>
> (a) freedom of conscience and religion;
>
> (b) freedom of thought, belief, opinion and expression, including freedom of the press and other media of communication;
>
> (c) freedom of peaceful assembly; and
>
> (d) freedom of association.[1]

But today those virtues are being challenged by courts, culture, and even legislation. New laws, cultural pressures, and digital surveillance all raise the same uneasy question: how much freedom do we still truly have, and how much are we willing to defend?

In the fall of 2025, Canadians had a strong awakening in this area when a flurry of bills were swiftly tabled in Parliament.

C-2, referenced as the Border Security bill, if passed without amendment, would have allowed the government to open mail without a warrant and limit cash transactions to $10,000 or less.[2] C-9 would expand hate speech legislation to be broader and take it out of the Attorney General's hands and put it into the Ministry of Justice's, effectively making it easier to weaponize for political reasons, putting Canadians who are offside with the government of the day in a vulnerable position.[3] C-8, referred to as the Telecommunications Bill, would give the federal government the power to cut phone lines and internet connections for those whom they deem to be a threat.[4]

Freedom is not a guarantee; it is an inheritance that must be protected.

THE FRAGILE NATURE OF LIBERTY

History shows that freedom rarely disappears all at once—it erodes in increments. A rule here, a restriction there, justified as "for our safety" or "for the public good." Over time, people adjust. They stop noticing the loss. Socialist and communist nations show us, vividly, that once a nation crosses over these kinds of thresholds, democracy is chilled and abuses begin to roll out. It is much easier to stop these legislative trends in advance than to try to change them once they have already been implemented. The price of liberty truly is eternal vigilance.

WHY FREEDOM MATTERS

Freedom is not only about politics—it is about human dignity. The ability to speak, think, worship, and raise one's family according to conscience lies at the heart of what it means to be fully human.

These rights are not inventions of modern governments; they are grounded in the idea that truth exists, that people have moral agency, and that citizens, not rulers, are ultimately responsible for their choices. The same worldview that inspired Canada's founders taught that individuals are endowed with inherent worth and the capacity for self-government.

Even those who are not religious benefit from these convictions. The freedom to disagree, to innovate, to create, and to challenge authority has been the engine of progress in every free society. Remove that freedom, and prosperity withers.

EROSION FROM WITHIN

Freedom does not usually fall to invading armies—it fades through neglect. When public discourse becomes dominated by fear of offence, universities punish debate, and professionals lose jobs for holding certain views, something deeper is wrong. The issue is not left versus right; it is open versus closed.

Consider the growing chill around discussions of family policy, parental rights, and moral questions once considered common ground. More and more Canadians self-censor to avoid controversy. The result is a quieter, more conformist culture—one in which people watch what they say rather than saying what they believe.

Freedom can survive disagreement. It cannot survive censorship.

THE ROLE OF LAW AND THE CHARTER

Canada's Charter of Rights and Freedoms, adopted in 1982, enshrined fundamental freedoms: conscience, religion, expression, assembly, and association. Yet the Charter also allows governments to limit those freedoms if they deem it "reasonable."[5] That clause, meant as a safeguard, has increasingly become a loophole. It can be argued that courts have at times deferred to government authority instead of protecting citizens from it.

The Charter's strength ultimately depends on citizens who understand it, invoke it, and defend it.

PARENTAL RIGHTS AND CONSCIENCE

One of the most contested freedoms today is the right of parents to direct their children's upbringing in accordance with their conscience and even to be informed about what is happening with their children at school.

This was dramatically illustrated in 2023, when the Premier of New Brunswick, Blaine Higgs, moved to remove a policy that would have allowed children to change their names and genders at school without informing their parents.[6]

Around the same time, there was an example of a minor in a New Brunswick town being put on hormone blockers at school without the consent of both parents. When Mom discovered the truth, she felt deeply hurt and violated that this had been kept from her as a caring, involved parent. The daughter later regretted her decision, wanted to detransition, and stated that she wished her mom had been included, as she might have discouraged her from doing it in the first place. Unfortunately, the daughter's puberty development had been interrupted, and her female body never fully returned.

As policies and stories like this emerged, the Higgs government decided to make adjustments.

A prominent national reporter, Vassy Kopelos, hosted Premier Higgs on her program when the news broke and challenged him on whether his policy move was truly supported by parents, or was it simply his own ideological agenda.[7] In response, a parental advocacy movement called *Don't Delete Parents* erupted, with tens of thousands of Canadians, many from New Brunswick, signing the petition backing the premier.[8]

This moment set off a domino effect, with other provincial leaders, such as the Minister of Education in Ontario, the Hon. Stephen Lecce, Premier Scott Moe (Saskatchewan), and then Premier Danielle Smith (Alberta), taking similar stances and some beginning to initiate policy changes.[9] Several polls indicated that these policies reflected the views of the majority of Canadians. Despite this, opposition was strong to what many felt, and still feel, was a very commonsense stance: that parents should never be 'deleted' from their children's lives by a government.

This cultural flashpoint illustrated one thing clearly: the role of parents in the lives of their own children cannot be taken for granted, and there are some who genuinely believe governments should be allowed to run interference on the communication lines between lovingly concerned parents and their children.

Strong families have always been the first school of character and citizenship, and the connection between parents and children is critical to the health and well-being of the next generation. When governments or institutions claim to know better than parents, society begins to unravel.

Respecting parental rights does not mean uniformity—it means acknowledging that parents, not bureaucrats, are closest to their children and most invested in their well-being. The state will never love a child as much as their own parents.

The same applies to conscience rights: doctors, teachers, or employees should never be forced to violate deeply held moral convictions in order to keep their jobs. A truly tolerant society protects even those it disagrees with.

THE RISE OF ANTI-FAITH BIGOTRY

Another troubling trend has been the casual dismissal—or open hostility—toward people of the Christian and Jewish faith. Churches and synagogues have been vandalized and burned to the ground with little national outcry or denunciation from prominent government leaders.[10] Good-willed pro-life and Christian charities have been seemingly targeted, and some have even lost charity status over minor technicalities such as missing a phone number on a form. One major political party banned pro-life Canadians from being able to run as candidates; mainstream media has vilified faith-based political candidates for their faith, and the list goes on.[11]

We must remember that freedom of religion was one of the first freedoms ever recognized in law. It paved the way for all the others. The right to believe, or not believe, without coercion is what separates a free nation from an authoritarian one. To erode that principle is to chip away at the foundation of every other liberty.

And while faith may make some uncomfortable, the values it embodies—dignity, forgiveness, service, compassion—are the very ones that keep our public life humane. Canadians should not be ashamed of that inheritance; they should cherish it.

RESPONSIBILITY AND RESTRAINT

Freedom without responsibility is chaos; responsibility without freedom is tyranny. The balance of both is what allows a society to flourish.

True freedom is not the right to do whatever we want—it is the right to do what is right, to act according to conscience and reason without fear of punishment. That requires restraint, maturity, and moral grounding. A society that loses that grounding will eventually trade freedom for control.

> *Freedom without responsibility is chaos; responsibility without freedom is tyranny.*

Protecting freedom, therefore, also means cultivating virtue: honesty, respect, courage, and service. Laws can defend freedom's boundaries, but only character can sustain it. Freedom is not inherited automatically; it is handed down through vigilance and courage. The generation that forgets to defend it will be the generation that loses it.

Our next chapter will explore another foundation of a strong society—the value of life itself—and why how we treat the most vulnerable among us reveals who we truly are as a nation.

TAKE 5

1. Freedom is not guaranteed—it must be guarded. For too long, Canadians have assumed our liberties were secure. Yet new laws, censorship, and cultural pressures reveal how fragile they are. Freedom, once lost, is rarely regained.

---

2. Liberty erodes slowly, not suddenly. History shows freedom rarely vanishes overnight—it fades through small compromises justified as "for safety" or "for the public good." Eternal vigilance remains the price of liberty.

---

3. Parental and conscience rights are under fire. Recent policies show how easily government can intrude on family and faith. Parents—not bureaucrats—know and love their children best, and no Canadian should be forced to violate conscience to keep a job.

---

4. Faith freedom is foundational. Freedom of religion paved the way for every other right. Dismissing or silencing faith communities weakens the moral framework that sustains democracy and compassion.

---

5. Freedom demands both courage and character. True liberty is not license—it's the ability to do what is right without fear. It survives only when citizens exercise virtue, vigilance, and restraint in equal measure.

EVERY
HUMAN BEING,
HOWEVER WEAK
OR WOUNDED,
BEARS THE
IMAGE OF GOD.

— CARDINAL BASIL HUME

CHAPTER 5

THE VALUE OF LIFE

When a society forgets the value of human life, everything else eventually unravels. Freedom, justice, and prosperity all rest on a single conviction—that every person has inherent worth. Lose that, and the rest cannot stand for long.

Canada is facing a quiet but profound moral crossroads. On one side is a tradition that recognizes life as sacred, purposeful, and deserving of protection. On the other side, there is a growing tendency to view life as negotiable—something valuable only when convenient, efficient, or desired. The outcome of this debate will define the kind of country we become, and leave to our children.

THE MEASURE OF A NATION

Every civilization is ultimately judged by how it treats its most vulnerable members. Whether we are talking about the unborn, the elderly, the disabled, or the mentally ill, compassion is tested where power meets weakness.

For generations, Canada sought to be a country that protected the vulnerable. We built hospitals, social programs, and safety nets. We prided ourselves on kindness. But over time, it would appear compassion has been confused with convenience. Rather than protecting life, we have increasingly rationalized ending it.

ABORTION AT ANY POINT OF PREGNANCY

Few Canadians realize that our country has no legal restrictions on abortion at any stage of pregnancy.[1] Where there are no restrictions, anything is allowed.

We stand virtually alone among developed nations in this regard. Where most countries draw limits at viability, or before 20 weeks, Canada's absence of legal restrictions allows abortion up to the moment of birth.[2] This means a healthy child capable of living outside the womb can be terminated at a doctor's discretion.

Whatever one's view of the politics, this fact should give us pause. It raises profound questions about how we define personhood and compassion. It also reveals how far our laws have drifted from the moral instincts that once guided them. The truth is, most Canadians are not aware of Canada's legislative status on abortion—but when they are informed, even the most ardent pro-choice advocates often express discomfort.[3] The idea that the life of a fully formed child can be legally ended in our nation is hard for most to digest, especially since it is paid for by taxpayers. This is likely why it is rarely discussed. It is a very disturbing and inconvenient truth for those who are pro-choice.

Life is not a matter of convenience. It is a matter of principle. If we say that some lives are expendable, we teach that all lives are negotiable.

MEDICAL ASSISTANCE IN DYING

In 2016, Canada legalized Medical Assistance in Dying (MAiD) for those suffering intolerably from terminal conditions.[4] Many believed it would remain a limited, last-resort option. Since then, the criteria have expanded dramatically—first to those with chronic illnesses, and now moving toward inclusion of people with mental-health conditions by 2027.[5]

This shift has stunned ethicists around the world, with even the United Nations Committee on the Rights of Persons with Disabilities (CRPD) denouncing Canada's policies and recommending that Canada reverse course.[6]

When a country begins offering death as a solution to depression, loneliness, aging, or poverty, something fundamental has changed.

True compassion seeks to relieve suffering, not eliminate the sufferer. When we respond to despair with state-administered suicide rather than hope, we have lost our moral compass.

DIGNITY, NOT DESPAIR

Fundamental dignity does not come from controlling the timing of our death. It comes from being valued to the end—from knowing our lives still matter, even when frail or dependent.

Hospice care, community support, friendship, and faith-based outreach all embody a different kind of compassion. They say, *"You are not a burden; you belong and you are valued."*

We need more of that spirit in Canada. Our answer to suffering should be accompaniment, not abandonment.

THE SLIPPERY SLOPE OF DEHUMANIZATION

History teaches what happens when societies lose the sense of intrinsic worth, when people are treated as expendable—whether for their age, ability, or inconvenience—the moral guardrails fall away.

In the 1930s, before the full horror of the Holocaust, Germany began with the "right to die" for the terminally ill. Within a few years, it evolved into the state-sanctioned killing of the disabled, then the elderly, and eventually millions deemed "unfit." It began not with hatred, but with a utilitarian logic that placed efficiency over humanity.

History reminds us that ideas have trajectories. If we don't draw clear moral lines, others will move them for us.

A DAMAGING MESSAGE FOR THE NEXT GENERATION

Frontline advocates on this issue, such as Amanda Achtman of the *Dying to Meet You*

What may seem to be a personal decision, inconsequential to those around us, may be just the opposite.

project, have begun pointing out a chilling unintended consequence of MAiD.

In a recent interview, she explained that, increasingly, millennials are disclosing the trauma that accompanies the loss of a grandparent to assisted suicide. In many cases, grandparents are gone before their grandchildren or children know that they were even considering MAiD. When they discover that their grandparent's life was taken by their own choice, many say it leaves them feeling that they were not worth staying alive for. Amanda went on to explain that many millennials simply do not know how to process this feeling of rejection.[7]

All this, once again, underscores the importance of the family unit, our connectedness, and the urgency of considering future generations in our decisions. What may seem to be a personal decision, inconsequential to those around us, may be just the opposite. Only time will tell what the sustained mental impacts of MAiD on loved ones will be, how those impacts will influence future generations, their relationships, social well-being, and productivity.

WHY LIFE MATTERS TO FREEDOM

The right to life is the first right; every other freedom depends on it. If governments decide when life begins or ends based on convenience, they also assume the power to decide whose life is worth protecting. Freedom cannot survive that logic.

Former generations understood this connection. The belief that people possess inherent worth—not because of wealth, race, or ability, but simply because they are human—is what grounds equality under the law. Remove that foundation, and equality becomes an illusion.

Protecting life, therefore, is not merely a religious conviction; it is the cornerstone of human rights.

A CULTURE THAT VALUES LIFE

Re-establishing a culture of life will take more than legislation. It requires rebuilding respect, one relationship at a time. It means valuing the elderly neighbour, the newborn, the child with special needs, and the struggling single parent. It means businesses, churches, and communities stepping forward to provide tangible support so that choosing life is both possible and practical.

Every time a community rallies around a family in crisis, every time a young mother receives help instead of judgment, every time we sit beside someone in pain instead of walking away—we push back against a culture of death.

HOPE FOR THE FUTURE

Despite the darkness of current trends, there are reasons for hope. Medical professionals, volunteers, and organizations across the country are quietly living out a different story—one of compassion rooted in care. Pregnancy resource centres, palliative-care teams, mental-health advocates, and faith-based charities remind us daily that love still changes outcomes.

We can choose that path as a nation. We can choose to value life at every stage and circumstance. We can choose to be a country where compassion means standing beside those who suffer, not writing them off. Together, we can turn the tide and make a difference. A nation that values life values everyone. When we defend the dignity of the smallest and the weakest, we defend our own humanity as well.

The next chapter will explore how culture itself—through media, education, and technology—shapes the moral direction of a nation, and why winning the cultural conversation is just as vital as winning political debates.

TAKE 5

1. Life is the foundation of every freedom. When a nation forgets the sanctity of life, freedom, justice, and prosperity all begin to crumble. Every right we cherish rests on the conviction that every person has inherent worth.

---

2. Compassion must never become convenience. Abortion without limits and the expanding reach of assisted death reveal a dangerous confusion between mercy and expedience. True compassion protects the vulnerable—it doesn't eliminate them.

---

3. Dignity means being valued to the end. Our worth is not determined by health, age, or ability. Real care means walking with those who suffer, not abandoning them. Hospice, community, and faith-based compassion are the antidotes to despair.

---

4. History warns where devaluing life leads. When societies lose sight of human worth, they slide toward utilitarianism and dehumanization. The first step down that path is always the redefinition of whose life "matters."

---

5. A culture of life begins with us. Rebuilding respect for life requires courage, care, and community—supporting families, honouring the elderly, and standing with the vulnerable. A nation that values life values everyone.

POLITICS IS DOWNSTREAM FROM CULTURE.

— ANDREW BREITBART

CHAPTER 6

CULTURE AT THE CROSSROADS

Every generation inherits a culture it did not create—and shapes the one that will follow. Culture is the unseen current that determines what a society believes, celebrates, and ultimately becomes. It defines what we teach our children, how we treat one another, and even what we believe is possible.

Today, Canada stands at a cultural crossroads. As we have discussed in previous chapters, principles that once undergirded our everyday life—truth, respect, responsibility, faith, family, and freedom—are being challenged by new narratives that often reject those very foundations. The question before us is simple: will we pass on a culture that strengthens or weakens the nation we love?

THE POWER OF INFLUENCE

Culture isn't shaped in Parliament first; it's shaped in classrooms, living rooms, and the digital spaces where people spend their time. Art, film, social media, entertainment, education—all of these inform the moral imagination of a people.

> *Culture isn't shaped in Parliament first; it's shaped in classrooms, living rooms, and the digital spaces where people spend their time.*

For decades, we've seen how cultural storytelling influences cultural trends and that can influence law and policy. Attitudes toward family, faith, and freedom have shifted not because of one election, but because of a steady stream of messages that redefined what is considered good, normal, or admirable. The people who tell the stories eventually write the rules.

This is why those who hold to strong, time-tested values cannot afford to abandon culture to others. If we retreat from film, music, journalism, or education, we surrender the conversation that shapes the next generation.

FROM SHARED TRUTH TO "MY TRUTH"

One of the most significant cultural shifts of our time is the move from shared truth to personal truth. "You have your truth, and I have mine" sounds tolerant, but it leaves society without a common compass.[1] Without truth, justice becomes arbitrary, science becomes politicized, and debate becomes impossible.

In earlier eras, Canadians—even when they disagreed—shared a moral baseline: honesty was good, family was vital, freedom was precious, and human life carried dignity. Today, those once-common convictions are often treated as optional or even outdated.

A culture cannot flourish without some agreed-upon standards. We need the courage to say that truth exists and that it matters—not to dominate others, but to build a society anchored in reality rather than emotion.

THE FAMILY: CULTURE'S FIRST SCHOOL

Long before there were governments or universities, there was the family. It is where children first learn trust, discipline, responsibility, teamwork, and love. When families are strong, communities thrive. When families fracture, every other institution feels the strain.

Yet family itself has become contested terrain. Economic pressures, overwork, and cultural messages that devalue marriage and parenthood are taking a toll. Many young adults feel uncertain about whether a stable family life is even achievable.

Supporting families is not just social policy—it's nation-building.[2] Tax systems, housing markets, and work-life balance should all encourage parents to raise children, not punish them for doing so.

THE IMPORTANCE OF HAVING BABIES

Demographics show that once a nation falls below a 2.1 birth rate, it is on its way to extinction.

A nation's birth rate plays a vital role in its long-term survival, sustainability, and prosperity. Demographers use the "replacement fertility rate"—typically around 2.1 children per woman in developed countries—as the threshold at which a population exactly replaces itself from one generation to the next without immigration.[3]

When fertility falls significantly below that level, fewer young people enter the workforce, leaving a shrinking base to support an ageing population, strained public services (such as pensions and healthcare), and lower economic vitality. For example, the global fertility rate fell from about five births per woman in 1950 to 2.3 in 2021 and is projected to continue downward to the replacement level of 2.1 and below. [4]

A healthy birth rate thus underpins steady generational renewal, economic activity, innovation, and the balance of dependency between young, working, and retired citizens.[5]

When birth rates remain well below the replacement level for extended periods, recovery becomes difficult, and the risk of irreversible demographic decline rises—posing serious challenges to national sustainability and prosperity. Many countries now have fertility rates well under 2.1, with some in Europe and East Asia dipping as low as 1.3 or below. At this point, unless offset by very large immigration or dramatic fertility rebound (which historically has proven elusive), the working-age population shrinks, economic growth stalls, public debt burdens grow, and national resilience is weakened.[6] The moment a country enters "ultra-low" fertility territory, the clock starts ticking—without enough births, a nation can struggle to generate the workforce, the tax base, and the generational vitality required to sustain its institutions and preserve prosperity.[7]

It is imperative that we foster a culture that upholds the importance of family and parenting, and that we elect leaders committed to policies which promote and sustain family growth. Lastly, honouring family and passing this understanding on is vital. Beyond policy, we each have a part to play: mentoring young couples, investing time in our kids, and honouring our elders. Strong families form strong citizens; strong citizens sustain free nations.

EDUCATION AND THE BATTLE FOR MINDS

Education was once about teaching students how to think. Increasingly, it is about telling them what to think.[8] Across the Western world, classrooms have become battlegrounds over ideology and identity. Students are encouraged to challenge every inherited truth, except those that the system prefers.

Canada's educators work hard and care deeply, but they need support to ensure schools remain places of learning, not indoctrination. As already discussed, parents have both the right and responsibility to be involved—to know what their children are being taught and to insist that differing perspectives be respected.

When curiosity is replaced by conformity, the next generation loses the ability to innovate and lead. A free society must protect freedom of inquiry in its schools, or it will lose freedom everywhere else.

MEDIA AND TECHNOLOGY

Never before have Canadians been so connected—and yet so divided.[9] Algorithms now curate what we see, rewarding outrage over understanding. A handful of tech companies wield more influence over opinion than any newspaper or broadcaster ever did.

This new reality demands discernment. We must learn to verify before sharing, to seek out multiple sources, and to teach our children how to navigate an online world that profits from their attention. Freedom of speech means little if people are quietly herded into digital echo chambers.

Citizens who value liberty must become intentional consumers of information—supporting independent journalism, creating honest content, and refusing to reward manipulation with clicks. The antidote to propaganda is participation.

THE IMPORTANCE OF SPIRITUAL AWAKENING

Even among those who do not consider themselves religious, there is a growing hunger for meaning, and spiritual awakening. Material success and entertainment cannot fill the more profound need for purpose. The decline of faith institutions has left a vacuum that politics and pop culture are ill-equipped to fill.

Re-engaging the moral and spiritual dimension of life is not about imposing belief; it's about restoring vitality.[10] Canada's freedoms, compassion, and sense of justice were all shaped by an understanding that right and wrong exist, that individuals are accountable, and that human dignity is fundamental. A society that forgets those truths drifts into cynicism and control.

We should not be ashamed of our faith heritage. Values rooted in the biblical call to love one's neighbour, to tell the truth, live accountably, and to steward our world have served everyone well—believers and non-believers alike.

REBUILDING THE CULTURAL GROUND

Changing culture begins where you are. It happens when a parent reads to a child, when a musician writes a song that uplifts, and speaks life rather than degrades, when a business owner chooses integrity over expedience, and when a citizen tells the truth even when it's unpopular. Movements start small: one conversation, one classroom, one community at a time.

Canadians who believe in freedom, responsibility, and compassion must reclaim cultural spaces with creativity, not complaint. The goal is not to shout louder, but to shine brighter. Culture is not a spectator sport. It belongs to those who participate. If we care about the Canada our children will inherit, we must step into the conversation with clarity, creativity, courage, and grace.

Now that we have discussed some of the key cultural trends and social issues of our times that desperately need the engagement of caring citizens, in the final chapters, we will begin to discuss simple action points that anyone who cares about the issues covered in this book can do.

Though the tides are intense, we are not powerless, and our greatest days as a nation, and a society, can still be ahead of us.

TAKE 5

1. Culture shapes everything—and everyone. Politics may write the laws, but culture writes the hearts. What we create, teach, and celebrate today will determine what kind of nation our children inherit tomorrow.

---

2. Truth must anchor our culture. The shift from shared truth to "my truth" has left society without a compass. Real freedom and justice depend on acknowledging that truth exists—and living by it with courage and humility.

---

3. Strong families sustain strong nations. Family is culture's first school. Nations thrive when they honour marriage, support parents, and value children. Falling birth rates and fractured homes threaten not just families, but the future itself.

---

4. Minds and media matter. Education and technology now shape beliefs more than pulpits or parliaments. We must champion curiosity, integrity, and discernment—teaching the next generation to think critically, not conform blindly.

---

5. Cultural renewal starts with us. Reviving our culture begins in homes, classrooms, studios, and businesses—where people choose integrity, truth, and creativity over fear and apathy. The goal is not to shout louder, but to shine brighter.

ALONE WE CAN DO SO LITTLE; TOGETHER WE CAN DO SO MUCH.

— HELEN KELLER

CHAPTER 7

BUILD SMART, BUILD TOGETHER

There is strength in conviction, but there is power in coordination.

In every era, meaningful change has come when individuals who care about the same principles link arms, and act in concert. The challenge for our generation is not the absence of good people; it is the absence of coordinated movement.

THE POWER OF UNITY

Canadians are known for politeness, but sometimes, our politeness turns into passivity. We hesitate to collaborate across denominational, regional, or ideological lines, fearing disagreement. Yet unity does not mean uniformity. It means different people working toward a common good.

Movements are built not by those who agree on everything, but by those who agree on what matters most.

When farmers, teachers, entrepreneurs, and pastors align around freedom, family, and responsibility, they form a moral and civic backbone that no government can ignore.

Movements are built not by those who agree on everything, but by those who agree on what matters most.

LESSONS FROM OTHER COMMUNITIES

Across Canada, many cultural and ethnic communities understand this principle well.

They identify promising leaders, help them secure nominations, and ensure their members show up at the polls.[1] They meet regularly, share information, and speak with one voice on issues that affect their families and livelihoods. There is nothing improper about this. It is democracy functioning as designed.

Recently, I had a friend close to the Premier of one of our most influential provinces tell me that for every one invitation the Premier gets from the Christian faith community, they get several dozen more from other communities. As a Christian, I was deeply convicted by this. Other faith communities and newer Canadians understand the importance of intentional and sustained civic engagement. They treasure the privilege of democracy and they engage deeply because they see its value.[2] Good for them. Every Canadian should be challenged by this example.

Building a better tomorrow begins with engagement, is strengthened by networks, and grows through consistent participation. The lesson is simple: presence is powerful, and organization multiplies influence.

THE EXAMPLE OF 4 MY CANADA

4 My Canada is one of the faith-based groups in our nation that understands the power and importance of grassroots engagement. For decades, 4 My Canada has been taking teams of next-generation leaders to Parliament to meet with elected officials, tracking the issues of the day, encouraging the network to be a voice, and connecting members with candidates who reflect their values of faith, family, freedom, and fiscal stewardship.

In Chapter Two, we discussed how, in the 2025 federal election, the organization helped dispatch more than 1,300 volunteers into 75 critical ridings to support quality candidates. Fourty-six of those candidates won. In that election, the winning party (the Liberal Party of Canada) missed getting a majority by only three seats.

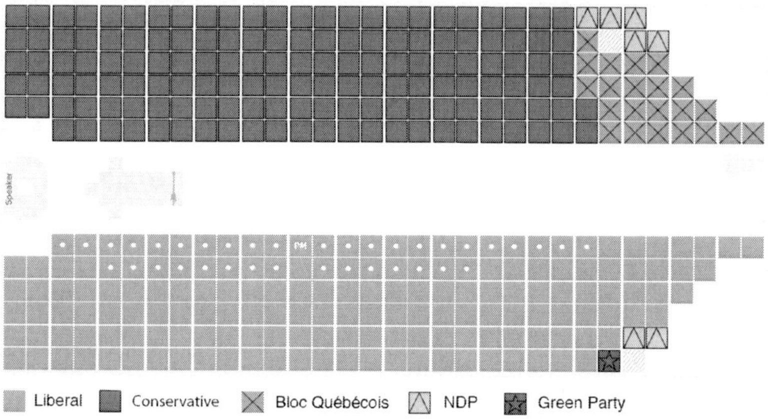

Source: Parliament of Canada, Our Commons Floorplan

Had these volunteers not shown up to help the candidates who reflected their views, the outcome would likely have been dramatically different. The above seat map shows just how close it was. If the two NDP and one Green Party seats on the bottom part of this image had been Liberal, we would have a dramatically different power dynamic in Parliament today.

Furthermore, the organizations post-election analysis indicated that if only 244 additional volunteers had been deployed into the right ridings, the election outcome would likely have been completely different, with the Conservative Party possibly winning.

Those who invested their time—whether door-knocking, phone-calling, or making coffee in a campaign office—had a tangible return. These volunteers proved that change is in the hands of those who show up in moments that matter.

Imagine that same model multiplied: local hubs in every province, united by common purpose and mutual respect. That is how grassroots turns into national renewal.

THE ROLE OF FAITH NETWORKS

Churches and many faith-based organizations already have what every movement needs—community, communication channels, and compassion. When believers see civic engagement as an extension of loving their neighbour, they have massive potential to become a stabilizing influence in public life. This is not about forcing values on others; it is about responsible civic engagement and getting involved just as other communities, faith, and interest groups do. When congregations encourage members to vote, volunteer for those that represent their values, and lead with integrity, they bless the entire nation, not just their own circle.

Furthermore, it is worth highlighting that success isn't merely measured by elections won, but by citizens awakened in faithful service and communities talking about duty, truth, and hope. It's the teacher who starts a civic club at school, the business owner who mentors a young leader, the pastor who hosts a candidate forum without partisanship.

The most significant movements in history began with small groups who refused to give up. Canada's future will not be shaped by the most enormous crowds, but by the most committed communities.

In the next chapter, we will outline even more practical ways we can all get involved, so that each and every one of you who is stirred by the pages of this book, can easily become part of the change our nation needs.

TAKE 5

1. Conviction matters—but coordination multiplies impact. When principled citizens act together, even small groups can shift the direction of a nation.

---

2. Unity is not uniformity. We don't need to agree on everything to work toward the common good. When people from different backgrounds rally around shared values—faith, family, and freedom—they form a moral force that cannot be ignored.

---

3. Engagement beats apathy. Some communities model this well: they organize, identify leaders, and show up. Their example should challenge every Canadian to steward the privilege of democracy with intentional participation.

---

4. Grassroots organization changes outcomes. The 4 My Canada example proves it—when ordinary citizens volunteer, mobilize, and work strategically, they can determine elections and shape policy. Presence and coordination turn conviction into measurable impact.

---

5. The Church can lead by serving. Faith networks already have what every movement needs—community, communication, and compassion. When believers engage civically out of love for neighbour, they strengthen the whole nation and model servant leadership in action.

THE SUCCESS OF THE

BIG SOCIETY

WILL DEPEND ON

THE DAILY DECISIONS

OF MILLIONS OF PEOPLE —

ON THEM GIVING THEIR

TIME, EFFORT, EVEN MONEY,

TO CAUSES AROUND THEM.

— DAVID CAMERON

CHAPTER 8

A PRACTICAL ROAD MAP

AND THE MOST IMPORTANT ACTION

Conviction without action changes little.

The good news is that, as we have illustrated throughout this book, changing a nation does not require celebrity, wealth, or permission—just willingness. Ordinary Canadians who care enough to act have always been the quiet force behind every meaningful change our country has known.[1] Getting involved looks different for everyone, but the key is the same: *start somewhere, start soon, and stay steady.*

Please consider one or all of these exciting opportunities and apply them to your life, family, and community.

BE INFORMED AND INTENTIONAL

Awareness is the foundation of effective action.

You have already demonstrated that you are committed to being informed by virtue of the fact that you are reading this book—way to go! The reality is that many citizens can name every sports team but not their local Member of Parliament, provincial representative, or mayor. If we want to shape our future, we must start by becoming students of the moment we are in. Here are a few easy ways you can do that.

- **Know your representatives.** Figure out who your MP, MLA, mayor, and councillors are. Once you do, get on their newsletter mailing lists, show up at their events, book a meeting with them, build a relationship with them and serve them—especially if they are tangibly working for things that you care about.

- **Understand the process.** Learn how government works at the federal, provincial, and municipal levels—and when key decisions are made. There are tons of resources on the internet which can help you with this.

- **Track spending.** Read your province's budget summary. Know where your tax dollars go, and reward leaders who manage responsibly by sending a kind note and volunteering for them in future campaigns.

- **Follow smart.** Whoever you are, there are citizen action groups that value the same things you do. Find out who they are, and get on their email lists and/or follow them on social media. They are doing the work for you, and great advocacy groups will not only keep you up to date on what is happening but also provide easy and effective action steps you can take. If you resonate with the positions that I have advocated for in this book so far (and I hope you do!), here are a few civic political action organizations I suggest you begin following:

- **4 My Canada**—Faith-based advocacy focused on faith, family, freedom, and fiscal stewardship (primarily federal, but not only). They specialize in issue-based advocacy, next-generation leadership training and election mobilization. www.4mycanada.com
- **Right Now**—A pro-life political action group focused on getting pro-life Canadians elected to office nationwide. www.itstartsrightnow.ca
- **ARPA Canada**—Faith-based advocacy specifically serving the Reformed denomination and tracking a variety of issues. www.arpacanada.ca

- **Canada Family Action**—A faith-based non-profit focused on mobilizing, training, and activating Canadians to defend Christian principles in Canadian society. www.familyaction.ca
- **Campaign Life Coalition**—Another pro-life political action group primarily serving the Canadian Catholic community nationwide and also specializing in strategic election engagement. www.campaignlifecoalition.com
- **Canadian Taxpayers Federation**—A civic action group focused on informing Canadians on how governments are stewarding our tax dollars and giving meaningful action points. www.taxpayer.com

Getting connected with these groups will help get your civic engagement skis pointed in the right direction. Sign up for their email lists today so that you don't miss a thing.

IN SECURE RIDINGS, SHOW UP EARLY IN NOMINATIONS

In ridings that are not "battle zones", meaning they pretty much always go to the same party, by the time a general election arrives, it is too late to make a real impact. Why is that? It is because whoever is the candidate for the favoured party is likely going to win, no matter how you vote at election time. This means that whoever votes at the nomination level, early in the process, really matters. What many people do not realize is that these candidates often win by only a few dozen votes. Your vote will almost always have the most significant impact during the nomination phase.

Think of nominations as the seed stage of democracy: if good people plant good seed there, good leadership grows later.

During the general election, your vote might be one out of tens of thousands. During a nomination, your vote will likely be one out of only hundreds. Your return on investment for civic engagement is much higher in nominations than anywhere else. The same can be said for party leadership races. They profoundly matter.

This is the clincher, though: only active members of a party can vote for its candidate or leader. Wise citizens will ensure that they have an active membership in the party that represents their views and values—especially if it is the favoured one in that riding.

Be advised that nomination races are often called spontaneously, especially if a snap general election is being anticipated. If your membership is not up to date, you can't vote. Sometimes they are called quietly, and only those with up-to-date memberships who are paying attention may catch them. If you care about who leads, join a political party and participate in the nomination process, get that membership and watch your emails. It costs little but counts for much.

THE MOST IMPORTANT ACTION

Volunteer strategically—spend your time where it matters <u>most</u>.

If you remember one thing from this entire book, remember this: the single most effective way to influence your nation's future is to volunteer in a tight race for a candidate who represents your values.

Campaigns are powered by ordinary people who decide to help. One steady, reliable volunteer can shift hundreds of votes—and, in some races, that's enough to change the outcome.

A candidate that you are helping doesn't need to be in your own riding. They might be thirty minutes away—or three provinces away. If the candidate in your area is already secure, invest your time where it counts most: in another close race that could go either way. You can do that by travelling to their riding to help them in person, or by making phone calls from anywhere in Canada.

...the single most effective way to influence your nation's future is to volunteer in a tight race for a candidate who represents your values.

In Canada, politics is a team sport. It's not enough for your personal candidate to win, they need teammates to get elected too. If more of their like-minded colleagues win, they will have a stronger coalition in Parliament and be able to advance legislation much more effectively. Team is everything. Your time and talent are limited—make sure you invest them where they'll produce the greatest return, and that is always in a tight race.

Volunteering is not as daunting as it may seem. It can be a lot of fun, especially if you do it with friends, or with the intent to make friends—because you always do! Serving can look like making phone calls or knocking on doors, delivering signs, helping with data entry, providing childcare or meals for campaign staff, hosting small fundraising events, or simply sharing accurate information online. There is always a way you can serve, and it will mean so much to the candidate and their core team.

If you're unsure where to start, organizations such as 4 My Canada and Right Now connect people of faith and conviction with strategic campaigns across the country.

DONATE

Democracy runs on participation—and yes, financial resources. Small, regular contributions from many people make a real impact. Consider becoming a monthly partner with an advocacy organization or political party that represents your views and values. Donating financially gives these organizations strength and gives you ownership in their movement.

Even modest, consistent giving enables work to continue between election cycles and, over time, makes a huge difference.

BEYOND THE BALLOT BOX

Additionally, civic influence doesn't end on election day. It includes letters to representatives, participation in consultations and local riding associations, attending town-hall meetings, serving on boards, and simply being visible. Politicians listen to the people who consistently show up. If you want your values represented, be present where decisions are made.

One of the most effective ways to make a difference is by serving on the board of your local riding association for the political party that best reflects your views and values. Doing so gives you a direct voice at the table in your community and opens doors to build meaningful relationships with your local candidate, potential future candidates, and other community leaders. Leaders naturally listen to those they know and trust—proximity is powerful.

When the opportunity arises, make it a priority to attend policy conventions and, if possible, serve on policy boards. Legislative ideas that exist as party policies today often become the laws of tomorrow. By suggesting policy ideas and signing up as a voting delegate, you can actively support the policies you believe in—and stand against those you don't. Getting involved with your local riding association for the party that best aligns with your values is an excellent way to begin this journey.

Never underestimate the power of sharing your perspective with your elected representative. Political staffers often note that for every one person who writes or calls about an issue, they assume there are another thousand in the riding who feel the same way. Tragically, so few take the time to reach out—so when you do, your voice truly carries weight.

Secondly, use this as a rule: the more effort it takes you to do, the greater the impact it will have. Something is always better than nothing. Sign petitions, send emails, post on social media—do it all! But the thing that will have the most significant impact is picking up the phone and calling your elected official's office, visiting in person, or attending a community event to share your views directly with your representative.

If you share your views in person, kindly, respectfully and in honour, it will have a tremendous impact.

USE YOUR VOICE WITH RESPECT AND COURAGE

Share your voice, views and quality information on your social media platforms, write a news article and engage on other communication platforms in an honourable way. This will help build a positive culture of civic awareness and healthy engagement. When you model courage and kindness, it will impact those around you and encourage them to do the same. Speak up when silence seems easier. Defend the rights of others—even when you disagree with them. Freedom flourishes when citizens pair courage with civility.

STRENGTHEN FAMILIES AND COMMUNITIES

Politics is downstream from culture, and culture is downstream from family. Strong homes make strong nations. Prioritize time at home, and mentor younger families. Support policies that value marriage, parenthood, and stability. Serve in your community—coach, volunteer, build relationships across divides.

When local bonds are strong, national unity follows. The neighbour who trusts your integrity locally is more likely to listen when you speak nationally.

Movements don't grow by accident. They grow because people organize. Begin to seek out like-minded individuals in your church and larger community, get in a room and talk about how you can be a positive change for your community. Ten people in a living room can become hundreds over time. Stay connected using group chats, social media or newsletters to share updates and opportunities. Finally, identify, support and develop leaders in your midst. If the party you support doesn't have a candidate who reflects your values, consider running yourself—or find someone who does, encourage them to run, and get behind them.

BUILD AND SUPPORT LIFE-AFFIRMING WORK

A society that values life values everyone. Support organizations that serve the vulnerable—whether crisis pregnancy centres, mental health services, or palliative care programs. Join the mailing lists of advocacy groups that protect life and dignity so you can stay informed and take timely action. If you see impactful media on a topic you care about—whether a film, article, or post—share it. Awareness multiplies compassion.

BE A CREATOR

Culture shapes so much. Use your talents—music, writing, business, education—to reflect the values that will contribute to a strong society. Let your creative talents flow. Additionally, support other creators and media outlets committed to honesty and accuracy.

SUPPORT FREE INSTITUTIONS AND INDEPENDENT VOICES

Freedom endures when citizens sustain the institutions that protect it.

Support independent media, charities, non-profits, and educational platforms that champion open debate. They need your participation and encouragement as much as your donations.

MENTOR AND MOBILIZE THE NEXT GENERATION

Invite younger Canadians into the story.

Share this book with them—many do not know the importance of balancing a budget, defending freedom, protecting all human life and how so few can have such a determining impact.

Let them shadow you at civic events, campaign offices, or community meetings. Show them that engagement is normal, not exceptional—this is how future leaders are born. A culture of participation is caught more than it's taught. If we want a hopeful Canada fifty years from now, we must build it through mentorship today.

PERSEVERE IN HOPE

Change is rarely instant. Whether you call it faith or conviction, perseverance is essential. Stay grounded in gratitude and hope. Refuse cynicism. Keep moving forward. Remember, the Canada we have today was built by those who got involved yesterday. Your consistent presence is powerful.

...the Canada we have today was built by those who got involved yesterday.

No matter what happens, if you do your best to show up time and time again, you will be able to look your children and grandchildren in the eyes and say, with integrity, that you fought to build a better nation for them.

If nothing else, your example of selfless service for their generation has the power to inspire them to do the same and effect change far beyond their lives. Always remember, your actions will have a ripple effect.

FOR PEOPLE OF FAITH: THE POWER OF PRAYER

I would be incredibly amiss if I did not mention the power and importance of prayer for our nation.

There are so many incredible national prayer movements in Canada, for which I am so grateful—find them and get involved. In them, you will find a beautiful community and synergy. Even better, start a prayer group for Canada in your own church or ministry.

I do want to say this, however, don't pray only. The model of Christ is both prayer and action. He started at the place of prayer, but He did not stop there. Jesus went to the mountain, then He went to the masses. He went to prayer, then to proclamation. He went to the Garden of Gethsemane, then to Golgotha. If Jesus had stopped at the place of prayer, there would be no way of salvation in the Christian faith. He got up out of the place of prayer and went to the Cross in the public square, literally.

Prayer is the undeniable starting point for people of the Christian faith, but it is never the ending point. If you are a person of faith, I invite you to arise with great love in your heart, beginning in the place of prayer, but like Jesus, ending in the place of action.

The greatest act of intercession creation has ever witnessed was not a prayer; it was an action. It was Christ, beaten and crucified in the public square, for those who could never pay Him back.

May we model the same love-inspired courage.

START SOMEWHERE

Don't wait for the perfect moment. Begin. Pick one level of government and follow its decisions for six months. Attend one council meeting or nomination vote. Volunteer a few hours for a candidate or cause that reflects your values. Support one organization that strengthens Canada's moral and civic foundations. Invite one friend or family member to join you. Just take the first step—you never know where it may lead, what doors it may open and if it could be the start of the fulfilment of your destiny!

Before we end our time together, I wanted to share one last story with you. I saved it until the end of this book because of the profound impact it had on my life. I hope, with all my heart, that it touches you as deeply as it touched me.

CHAPTER "ACTION" CHECKLIST

Ready to get going? Here is a 15-point check list from the suggestions in this chapter. If you start checking off the items on this list, you will be on your way in no time at all!

__ Identify your local MP, MLA, mayor, and councillors & subscribe to their updates.

__ Look up 2-3 advocacy groups in your areas of interest and subscribe to their updates.

__ Email 4 My Canada and let them know you want to be put on their volunteer list to help in swing ridings (email: admin@4mycanada.ca).

__ Attend community meetings whenever you can.

__ Volunteer in your representative's office to build authentic relationships.

__ Join a political party that represents your views.

__ Donate monthly to an advocacy group or a political party that represents your views and values.

__ Plan to vote in the nomination race for your local riding for the party that you most align with.

__ Plan to attend the next policy convention for the party that most represents your views and values.

__ Write an article about an issue you care about and submit it to your local paper. Forward it to your elected officials.

__ Pick one friend and bring them along with you!

__ Pick one next generation leader and bring them along with you too!

__ Pray for your local representatives at least one day a week, or start a prayer group for your community, province and/or nation.

__ Write a song, a poem, make a video or paint a painting to communicate a message about one of the themes of this book and share it with your community.

__ Model courage, respect and honour in all your communications and impact the culture around you!

EVIL TRIUMPHS WHEN GOOD MEN DO NOTHING.

— EDMUND BURKE

CHAPTER 9

THE NATION GOES TO THOSE WHO SHOW UP

Some moments are too impactful to forget; you can't un-experience them. They mark you.

A MOMENT ON PARLIAMENT HILL

I will never forget the day I stood on the steps of Parliament Hill with one of Canada's most cherished Christian leaders, David Mainse.[1] For decades, he was known as the gentle voice of 100 Huntley Street—a pioneer of Canadian Christian television. He spoke hope to millions, but he also understood something many overlooked: faith, civic engagement, and freedom are inseparable.

Thousands of us were gathered in front of the Peace Tower on Parliament Hill to pray for Canada. David was there with us and led with a beautiful exhortation and prayer. As always, he spoke with authenticity, gravity, and depth of wisdom. After his remarks, he walked over to where I was and told me a story.

He shared how, in 1989, under Prime Minister Brian Mulroney, a bill had passed the House of Commons that would have restricted abortion in Canada to cases where the mother's life was in danger. The previous law had been struck down by the Supreme Court of Canada in 1988, and the Court had then called upon Parliament to bring forward a new one.

After passing through the House of Commons, the bill went to the Senate, where the debate was fierce. When the final vote in the Senate was tallied, it was tied. Under Parliamentary rules, a tie vote meant the measure was defeated—this was the first time this had happened since 1941.

David relayed the story carefully and intently. He then said to me, with a tear beginning to trickle out of his eye, "You know, there were Senators who supported that bill—who agreed with it—but didn't show up to vote that day because of the pressure from both sides. The pro-abortion lobby was pressuring them to vote against it, but so were some pro-life groups who felt abortion should never be allowed, not even if the mother's life was in danger. If those Senators had shown up to vote the bill would have passed and millions more Canadians would be alive today."

With fatherly grief and compassion in his eyes, he looked directly at me and said, "The nation goes to those who show up to the meeting."

It was like an anvil hit my heart.

What struck me in that moment was that David was not speaking of a prayer meeting, though he was a man of deep prayer, and we were at one. He was speaking of a political meeting where people could cast a vote—a vote that could save lives.

It is worth taking a moment to unpack the magnitude of this moment's implications and how true David's assessment was.

According to the Canadian Institute for Health Information (2021), over 90% of reported abortions occur at or before 13 weeks, about 9% between 14–20 weeks, and fewer than 0.1% after 21 weeks. Very few of those are because of a threat to the mother's life.[2]

Statistics Canada has consistently estimated that 100,000 abortions happen each year in our nation. Due to incomplete reporting, it is widely understood that this figure is low.

In 36 years, this equates to 3.6 million Canadians. If born, many of those Canadians would now have children of their own, meaning the loss of life to abortion is actually significantly higher because of the loss of the children's children. 3.6 million is more than the population of all the Maritime provinces and Saskatchewan combined—5 entire Canadian provinces.[3] This is how many Canadians are missing because of one single vote, and it is an underestimation.

Attendance matters.

David's words hit me so deeply. I have never forgotten them.

I decided in that moment that every opportunity I had to show up to a meeting to vote for something I believe in, I would, and that I would take as many others as I could with me—knowing that you never know whose vote might be the "one".

David's statement wasn't just about politics; it was about responsibility.

Showing up doesn't always look glamorous, isn't always enjoyable (though it can be), and at times is costly. It means attending a meeting when you are tired, voting in a nomination when it's new, writing a letter when you don't quite know what to say, or standing quietly for what's right when everyone else has gone silent.

> ***David's statement wasn't just about politics; it was about responsibility.***

Most turning points in history were not decided by crowds, but by handfuls. In legislative chambers, school boards, and community halls, the course of nations has often shifted because a few people refused to stay home or self-censor.

THE TRAGEDY OF ABSENCE

The greatest threat to a free and moral nation is not always the wrongdoing of the few—it is the inaction of the many. When good people remain silent or disengaged, others fill the void.

James 4:17 says, *"If anyone, then, knows the good they ought to do and doesn't do it, it is sin for them."*[4] Whether one approaches that from faith or from ethics, the principle holds: responsibility avoided is still responsibility.

Every generation faces its own test. Ours is the temptation of apathy. Will we scroll, sigh, shake our heads—and then move on? Decisions that affect our freedoms, our families, and our children's future are being made by those who won't.

Being the change our world needs also means showing up for one another in loving, intentional community—for the single parent trying to make ends meet, for the student navigating a culture that mocks conviction, or for the elderly neighbour who feels forgotten. Societies flourish when citizens notice and engage.

I think of the abolitionists, suffragettes, reformers, and civic pioneers who built this country. Few were famous when they began. They were teachers, farmers, homemakers, and business owners who believed they could make a difference. They attended meetings. They wrote petitions. They organized. They showed up. And because they did, Canada became freer, fairer, and stronger.

Remember the lessons of those who came before us:

- The small group that ratified Canada's Confederation.
- The reformers who abolished slavery.

- The volunteers who gave hours that changed elections.
- The pastors and parents who stood for truth when it was unpopular.
- The citizens who showed up to meetings that no one else attended, and tipped the balance of history.

They were not extraordinary people. They were ordinary people who acted when the moment called for it.

Now it is our turn.

CONCLUSION

WHAT WE'VE LEARNED

Through these pages, we have learned the following powerful principles:

- **Stewardship matters.** A nation that spends recklessly—financially or morally—eventually runs out of both resources and respect.
- **Freedom matters.** It is the oxygen of democracy, fragile and precious.
- **Life matters.** Every life—young or old, strong or weak—bears dignity that no government can give or take away.

- **Culture matters.** The stories we tell today become the standards our children inherit tomorrow.
- **Engagement matters.** Elections and policies are shaped by the people who show up, not by those who merely observe.
- **Unity matters.** When citizens link arms across differences for the sake of what's right, they become unstoppable.
- **Faith matters.** Not as dogma to impose, but as a moral compass that has guided every lasting democracy in history.

These principles are the scaffolding of a healthy and principled civilization.

A GREAT HOPE

In closing, I want to say that I have great hope.

I have hope because YOU are still reading this book. You have not put it down, or returned it to the shelf before reading to the end.

Across the nation, people just like you and me are rediscovering the joy and power of civic life. Prayer groups, volunteer teams, and local movements are rising again. The same spirit that once built Canada's schools, hospitals, and democratic institutions is stirring—and you are a part of it.

And this is the reality: *our history is still being written.*

This means there is still hope for a better tomorrow if we do not grow weary in well-doing.

The gap between the Canada we have and the Canada we want will not be closed by fear, withdrawal, or anger, but by loving, courageous, and servant-hearted action that does not give up—one conversation, one meeting, one vote, and one commitment at a time.

IF NOT NOW, THEN WHEN

When I think back to that afternoon on Parliament Hill, I can still feel David Mainse's strong fatherly arm on my shoulder and hear his gentle but unshakable voice: *"The nation goes to those who show up."*

The question before us is timeless—and personal: *If not now, then when? If not us, then who?*

May we be the people who answer that question—not with slogans, but with our lives.

If this is all hitting you too, and you are willing to make the commitment to begin doing something, anything—if you are determined to show up—I invite you to write the words "Count Me In" on the next page.

Let your handwritten declaration stand as a lasting reminder of the choice you are making today—and may it serve as a testimony to your children, and their children, of your commitment to building a stronger nation for their future.

Every voice, volunteer, and vote matters.

Let's make it count.

MY WRITTEN COMMITMENT

(Please write "Count Me In" on this line if you are in.)

Your Signature

Date

ACKNOWLEDGEMENTS

Special thanks to the many incredible men and women on the frontlines of civic engagement in Canada who have mentored and inspired me over the years. You know who you are. Through your examples I have learned to "do more of what works", and it has made all the difference.

RECOMMENDED READING

Do Something! 365 Ways You Can Strengthen Canada
Preston Manning

Faith, Leadership and Public Life
Preston Manning

Building Prosperity in a Canada Strong and Free
Preston Manning

To Shift a Nation
Craig Docksteader

Church in Society
Don Hutchinson

We Have a Voice
Rob Parker

ENDNOTES

Epigraph

1. Order of Canada 50th Anniversary. (n.d.). *Motto of the Order of Canada.* https://www.orderofcanada50.ca/motto; The Bible. (n.d.). *Hebrews 11:16* (New International Version). https://www.biblegateway.com/passage/?search=Hebrews+11%3A16&version=NIV

Preface

1. Office of the Parliamentary Budget Officer. (2025, March). Economic and Fiscal Outlook – March 2025 (Report No. RP-2425-030-S). Government of Canada. https://www.pbo-dpb.ca/en/publications/RP-2425-030-S--economic-fiscal-outlook-march-2025--perspectives-economiques-financieres-mars-2025
2. Angus Reid Institute. (2024, October 3). Canadians divided on direction of country but remain optimistic about future. Angus Reid Institute. https://angusreid.org

Chapter 1

1. CBC News. (2022, February 22). *MP Mark Strahl claims single mom's bank account frozen for donating to convoy protest.* https://www.cbc.ca/news/canada/british-columbia/mp-mark-strahl-convoy-protest-briane-bank-account-frozen-1.6360132; Vancouver Sun. (2025, October 10). *B.C. nurses, doctors fired over vaccine refusal lose court bid to toss health orders.*https://vancouversun.com/news/local-news/b-c-nurses-doctors-fired-over-vaccine-refusal-lose-court-bid-to-toss-health-orders;Justice Centre for Constitutional Freedoms. (2025, May 2). B.C. *healthcare workers face another hurdle in COVID vaccine mandate challenge*. https://www.jccf.ca/bc-healthcare-workers-face-another-hurdle-in-covid-vaccine-mandate-challenge; Justice Centre for Constitutional Freedoms. (2025, October 1). Bill C-8 would allow minister to secretly cut off phone, internet service, CCF warns. https://theccf.ca/bill-c-8-would-allow-minister-to-secretly-cut-off-phone-internet-service-ccf-warns; Google. (2025, October 1). *Law experts warn Bill C-9 is an assault on free speech.* https://youtu.be/c8Mqyy05JbI

2. Editors of Science News Today. (2025, September 17). *The fall of Rome: Why the empire collapsed.* Science News Today. https://www.sciencenewstoday.org/the-fall-of-rome-why-the-empire-collapsed

3. Fraser Institute. (2025, October 10). *Canada's fiscal policy has undermined efforts to tackle inflation.* https://www.fraserinstitute.org/sites/default/files/canadas-fiscal-policy-has-undermined-efforts-to-tackle-inflation.pdf

Chapter 2

1. Wikipedia contributors. (2025, October 27). *Clapham Sect*. Wikipedia. https://en.wikipedia.org/wiki/Clapham_Sect

2. The King Center. (n.d.). *Martin Luther King Jr.* The King Center. https://thekingcenter.org/about-tkc/martin-luther-king-jr

3. Élections Québec. (1995, October 30). *1995 referendum on Québec's accession to sovereignty.* https://www.electionsquebec.qc.ca/en/results-and-statistics/1995-referendum-on-quebecs-accession-to-sovereignty/

4. Carter, O. (2025, August 19). *Tight races Canada 2025 federal election: Three ridings decided by under 50 votes.* CO24. https://co24.ca/tight-races-canada-2025

5. McMackon, C. (2025, May 10). *Recount sees Liberals take Quebec riding of Terrebonne by single vote.* Global News.https://globalnews.ca/news/11174218/terrebonne-recount-liberal-canada-election/

6. Wikipedia contributors. (2025, October 27). *2025 Canadian federal election.* Wikipedia. https://en.wikipedia.org/wiki/2025_Canadian_federal_election

7. Wikipedia contributors. (2025, October 27). *2025 Calgary municipal election.* Wikipedia. https://en.wikipedia.org/wiki/2025_Calgary_municipal_election

8. City of Beaumont. (2025, October 24). *Official 2025 municipal election results.* https://www.beaumont.ab.ca/news/official-2025-municipal-election-results

9. Global News. (2024, October 21). *New Brunswick election 2024 results: Hampton-Fundy-St. Martins.* https://globalnews.ca/news/10794826/new-brunswick-election-2024-results-hampton-fundy-st-martins/

10. Global News. (2024, October 21). *New Brunswick election 2024 results: Quispamsis.* https://globalnews.ca/news/10794827/new-brunswick-election-2024-results-quispamsis/

11. Wikipedia contributors. (2025, October 27). *32nd Alberta general election.* Wikipedia. https://en.wikipedia.org/wiki/32nd_Alberta_general_election

12. Wikipedia contributors. (2025, October 27). *2019 Canadian federal election.* Wikipedia. https://en.wikipedia.org/wiki/2019_Canadian_federal_election

13. Wikipedia contributors. (2025, October 27). *2013 Liberal Party of Canada leadership election.* Wikipedia. https://en.wikipedia.org/wiki/2013_Liberal_Party_of_Canada_leadership_election

14. Statistics Canada. (2025, October 25). *Voter turnout.* https://www.statcan.gc.ca/hub-carrefour/quality-life-qualite-vie/good-governance-saine-gouvernance/voter-turnout-participation-electorale-eng.htm
Statistics Canada. (2015, September 14). *Electoral participation in last provincial election.* https://www150.statcan.gc.ca/t1/tbl1/en/tv.action?pid=4510002601

15. 4 My Canada. (2022). *4mycanada.com*. 4 My Canada Association. Retrieved October 28, 2025, from http://www.4mycanada.com

Chapter 3

1. Debt.ca. (n.d.). *Canada debt clock*. Debt.ca. Retrieved October 28, 2025, from https://www.debt.ca/debt-clock

2. Debt.ca. (n.d.). *Newfoundland and Labrador provincial debt clock.* Debt.ca. Retrieved October 28, 2025, from https://www.debtclock.ca/provincial-debtclocks/newfoundland-and-labrador

3. Fuss, J., Hill, T., & Dunstan, W. (2025). *Federal and provincial debt-interest costs for Canadians, 2025 edition.* Fraser Institute. https://www.fraserinstitute.org/sites/default/files/2025-08/federal-and-provincial-debt-interest-costs-for-canadians-2025.pdf

4. Department of Finance Canada. (2024). *Annex 2: Debt Management Strategy.* Government of Canada. https://budget.canada.ca/2024/report-rapport/anx2-en.html

5. CP24. (2025, October 27). *Budget watchdog warns 'it's not a funny fiscal outlook'*. YouTube Shorts. https://www.youtube.com/shorts/XiU8mpfYF-g

6. Proverbs 22:7; 13:22 (King James Version). These verses illustrate financial principles regarding debt and inheritance.

7. Saillant, R., & Emery, H. (2019). *Is New Brunswick heading over the fiscal cliff?* Canadian Tax Journal, 67(4), 1011-1024.

8. Whalen, A., & Emes, J. (2023, March). *New Brunswick Premiers and Provincial Government Spending*. Fraser Institute. https://www.fraserinstitute.org/sites/default/files/NB-premiers-and-provincial-government-spending.pdf

9. Fraser Institute. (2025, January). *Measuring the fiscal performance of Canada's premiers*. https://www.fraserinstitute.org/sites/default/files/2025-01/measuring-fiscal-performance-of-canadas-premiers-2025-newsrelease-atlc.pdf; Fraser Institute. (2025, January). *New Brunswick premier Higgs tops among peers: Spending and tax policy.* https://www.fraserinstitute.org/commentary/new-brunswick-

premier-higgs-tops-among-peers-spending-and-tax-policy

10. MacMinn Varvos, M. (2021). Canada's immigration history: Milestones and stories. In A. Caldararu et al. (Eds.), *Canadian settlement in action: History and future* (Chapter 1, Section "Canada's Immigration History: Milestones and Stories"). NorQuest College. https://pressbooks.openeducationalberta.ca/settlement/chapter/canadas-immigration-history-milestones-and-stories/
11. Brewster, M. (2022, November 24). RCMP called to investigate multiple cases of veterans being offered medically assisted death. *CBC News*. https://www.cbc.ca/news/politics/veterans-maid-rcmp-investigation-1.6663885

Chapter 4

1. Department of Justice Canada. (n.d.). *The Constitution Acts, 1867 to 1982.* Government of Canada. Retrieved October 28, 2025, from https://laws-lois.justice.gc.ca/eng/const/page-12.html
2. Norton Rose Fulbright. (2025). *Bill C-2 in the*

House: Amendments to Customs Act and more to strengthen Canada's borders: Bill C-2: Major changes to Canada's Anti-Money Laundering regime. https://www.nortonrosefulbright.com/en/knowledge/publications/837c1c47/bill-c2-in-the-house-amendments-to-customs-act-and-more-to-strengthen-canadas-borders; https://www.nortonrosefulbright.com/en/knowledge/publications/3ef979fb/bill-c2-major-changes-to-canadas-anti-money-laundering-regime

3. Canadian Civil Liberties Association. (2025, September 22). *CCLA: Bill C-9 risks criminalizing peaceful protest.* https://ccla.org/press-release/ccla-bill-c-9-risks-criminalizing-peaceful-protest/

4. Israel, T. (2025, September 26). *Government needs to fix dangerous flaws in federal cybersecurity proposal.* Canadian Civil Liberties Association. https://ccla.org/privacy/fix-dangerous-flaws-in-federal-cybersecurity-proposal/

5. Government of Canada. (n.d.). *Guide to the Canadian Charter of Rights and Freedoms*. Canadian Heritage. Retrieved October 28, 2025, from https://www.canada.ca/en/canadian-heritage/services/how-rights-

protected/guide-canadian-charter-rights-freedoms.html

6. Jabri-Pickett, S. (2023, June 9). Canadian province changes LGBT policy in schools to 'recognize role of parents'. *Reuters*. https://www.reuters.com/world/americas/canadian-province-changes-lgbt-policy-schools-recognize-role-parents-2023-06-09/

7. Higgs, B. (2025, October 27). *New Brunswick Premier explains changes being made to Policy 713 on gender identity in schools* [Video]. YouTube. https://youtu.be/Kp3-t-ovvdM

8. Grasseschi, F. (2023). *Don't Delete Parents*. 4 MY Canada. https://www.dontdeleteparents.ca

9. Ontario Ministry of Education. (n.d.). *Education and training*. Government of Ontario. Retrieved October 28, 2025, from https://www.ontario.ca/page/education-and-training; Fraser Institute. (2024, November 1). *Expand school choice to help end controversies over gender and other issues.* https://www.fraserinstitute.org/commentary/expand-school-choice-help-end-controversies-over-gender-and-other-issues; National Observer. (2024, November

1). *Alberta Bill requires parental consent for students to change name or pronoun.* https://www.nationalobserver.com/2024/11/01/news/alberta-bill-parental-consent-students-name-pronoun

10. CBC News. (2023, July 26). *Church fires in Canada: Investigations underway.* https://www.cbc.ca/news/canada/church-fires-canada-investigation-1.6739117

11. Loewen, P. (2014, May 9). Trudeau's puzzling pro-choice dictum. *Ottawa Citizen*. https://ottawacitizen.com/news/politics/trudeaus-puzzling-pro-choice-dictum

Chapter 5

1. Courthouse Libraries BC. (2024, February 20). *Abortion rights in Canada.* https://www.courthouselibrary.ca/how-we-can-help/our-legal-knowledge-base/abortion-rights-canada

2. Charlotte Lozier Institute. (n.d.). *International abortion norms*. Retrieved October 28, 2025, from https://lozierinstitute.org/internationalabortionnorms/

3. We Need A Law. (2020, June 4). *Canadian opinions on abortion: Abortion polls summarized*. https://

weneedalaw.ca/2020/06/canadian-opinions-on-abortion/

4. Health Canada. (2024, October 28). *Medical assistance in dying: Legislation in Canada*. Government of Canada. https://www.canada.ca/en/health-canada/services/health-services-benefits/medical-assistance-dying/legislation-canada.html; Department of Justice Canada. (n.d.). *Part 1 – Description of legislation on medical assistance in dying*. Government of Canada. https://www.justice.gc.ca/eng/rp-pr/other-autre/ad-am/p2.html

5. Health Canada. (2024, October 28). *Medical assistance in dying: Legislation in Canada*. Government of Canada. https://www.canada.ca/en/health-canada/services/health-services-benefits/medical-assistance-dying/legislation-canada.html; Centre for Addiction and Mental Health (CAMH). (n.d.). *Medical Assistance in Dying (MAiD) and mental illness – FAQs*. https://www.camh.ca/en/camh-news-and-stories/maid-and-mental-illness-faqs

6. Canadian Affairs. (2025, March 30). *'Extremely concerned': UN tells Canada to stop Track 2 MAiD*. https://www.canadianaffairs.news/2025/03/30/

extremely-concerned-un-tells-canada-to-stop-track-2-maid/; Inclusion Canada. (2025, March 26). *"Do better" – Inclusion Canada welcomes UN Committee's concluding observations on Canada's disability rights record.* https://www.inclusioncanada.ca/post/do-better-inclusion-canada-welcomes-un-committee-s-concluding-observations-on-canada-s-disabilit

7. Scheidl, N., & Achtman, A. (2025, October 27). *Expansion of euthanasia to the mentally vulnerable?* [Video]. *Faytene.tv.* https://youtu.be/lWBK02FzngM

Chapter 6

1. Crul, S. (2024, October 17). *Perspectives on the post-truth era*. FreedomLab. https://www.freedomlab.com/posts/perspectives-on-the-post-truth-era;
   Wax, T. (n.d.). *Truth becomes referendum likes* [Blog post]. The Gospel Coalition. https://www.thegospelcoalition.org/blogs/trevin-wax/truth-becomes-referendum-likes/

2. Mitchell, P. J. (n.d.). *Envisioning a federal family-formation policy framework for Canada*. Cardus. https://www.cardus.ca/research/envisioning-a-federal-family-formation-policy-framework-for-canada/;

Evangelical Fellowship of Canada. (n.d.). *Family & community*. https://www.evangelicalfellowship.ca/Themes/Family-Community

3. United Nations, Department of Economic and Social Affairs, & Population Division. (2016). *Indicators of sustainable development: Methodology sheets, third edition* (Indicator: Total fertility rate) [PDF]. https://www.un.org/esa/sustdev/natlinfo/indicators/methodology_sheets/demographics/total_fertility_rate.pdf; Alkema, L., Raftery, A. E., Gerland, P., Clark, S. J., Pelletier, F., Buettner, T., & Heilig, G. K. (2011). Probabilistic projections of the total fertility rate for all countries. Demography, 48(3), 815–839. https://doi.org/10.1007/s13524-011-0040-5

4. United Nations Population Fund. (2023). *The 8 Billion Question: Too Many or Too Few?* [Report]. https://www.unfpa.org/swp2023/too-few

5. Statistics Canada. (2016, September 28). Dependency ratio (Catalogue no. 82-229-X). https://www150.statcan.gc.ca/n1/pub/82-229-x/2009001/demo/dep-eng.htm

6. Yanatma, S. (2024, September 28). *Europe's fertility crisis: Which European country is having the fewest*

*babies?*Euronews. https://www.euronews.com/health/2024/09/28/europes-fertility-crisis-which-european-country-is-having-the-fewest-babies; Ritchie, H. (2024, June 10). *Which countries have fertility rates above or below the "replacement level"?* Our World in Data. https://ourworldindata.org/data-insights/which-countries-have-fertility-rates-above-or-below-the-replacement-level

7. McKinsey Global Institute. (2025, January 15). *Dependency and depopulation? Confronting the consequences of a new demographic reality*. McKinsey & Company. https://www.mckinsey.com/mgi/our-research/dependency-and-depopulation-confronting-the-consequences-of-a-new-demographic-reality

8. Zwaagstra, M. (2022, December 5). *Woke ideology now dominates Ontario public schools*. Fraser Institute. https://www.fraserinstitute.org/commentary/woke-ideology-now-dominates-ontario-public-schools; Sikkema, J. (2025, February 20). *Resisting gender ideology indoctrination in Canada's public schools*. C2C Journal. https://c2cjournal.ca/2025/02/resisting-gender-ideology-indoctrination-in-canadas-public-schools/

9. Bridgman, A. (2022, May 29). *The role of social media in polarizing Canadians*. Centre for Media, Technology and Democracy. https://www.mediatechdemocracy.com/all-work/the-role-of-social-media-in-polarizing-canadians; Hutchinson, A. (2025, September 28). *Engagement-based algorithms are causing social division. But is there an alternative?* Social Media Today. https://www.socialmediatoday.com/news/social-media-algorithms-drive-division-angst-algorithmic-oversight/761323/

10. Long, K. N. G., Rosmarin, D. H., & Koh, H. K. (2024, September 10). *Bridging the spirituality and health gap to improve outcomes*. Harvard Public Health Magazine. https://harvardpublichealth.org/policy-practice/bridging-the-spirituality-and-health-gap-to-improve-outcomes; Health Affairs. (2023, September 6). *Spirituality as a determinant of health: Emerging policies, practices, and systems*. https://www.healthaffairs.org/doi/10.1377/hlthaff.2023.01643; The relationship between spirituality, health-related behavior, and psychological well-being. (2020). *National Center for Biotechnology Information.* https://www.ncbi.nlm.nih.gov/pmc/articles/PMC7457021/

Chapter 7

1. Wang, J., Levy, S., Wang, R., Kulshrestha, A., & Rabbany, R. (2020). SCG: Spotting coordinated groups in social media. *arXiv*. https://doi.org/10.48550/arXiv.1910.07130; Lachance, S., & Beauvais, E. (2024). Group-based affect and the Canadian party system. *Canadian Journal of Political Science/Revue canadienne de science politique*, 57(1), 1–18. https://doi.org/10.1017/S0008423923000719

2. Zhang, L., & Wang, X. (2023). *Functional metagenomics-guided discovery of potent Cas9 inhibitors in the human microbiome*. PubMed Central. https://www.ncbi.nlm.nih.gov/articles/PMC10625494/

Chapter 8

1. Manning, P. (2014, March 1). *What are the next steps?* Maclean's. https://www.macleans.ca/politics/ottawa/preston-manning-what-are-the-next-steps/; Canadian Policy Research Networks. (n.d.). *Public policy and social research in Canada*. https://oaresource.library.carleton.ca/cprn/18162_en.pdf; Canadian Centre for Policy Alternatives. (2025, February). Stoking the

fire: A policy analysis. https://www.policyalternatives.ca/wp-uploads/2025/02/MB-Stoking-Fire-v2-1.pdf; McDonald, M. (2022). *The politics of identity: A comparative analysis. Journal of Political Ideologies*, 27(3), 289–308. https://doi.org/10.1080/13504622.2022.2135688

Chapter 9

1. Mainse, D. (n.d.). *Biography*. David Mainse. https://www.davidmainse.com/biography; Crossroads Christian Communications Inc. (n.d.). *Rev. David Mainse*. https://crossroads.ca/about/rev-david-mainse/

2. Canadian Institute for Health Information. (2025, March 20). *Induced abortions in Canada*. https://www.cihi.ca/en/induced-abortions-in-canada

3. Statistics Canada. (2025, September 24). *Population estimates, quarterly* (Table 17-10-0009-01). https://www150.statcan.gc.ca/t1/tbl1/en/tv.action?pid=1710000901

4. The Holy Bible, New International Version. (2011). Zondervan.

ABOUT THE AUTHOR

For more than two decades, Faytene Grasseschi has been actively involved in political life at every level—nominations, leadership races, serving on riding boards, attending policy conventions, speaking to Parliamentary committees and working in general elections across federal, provincial, and municipal arenas. She has also sought political office three times—winning once in a nomination race and coming remarkably close to victory in the other two after leading strong campaigns that earned widespread respect.

Nationally, she has led issue campaigns which have inspired Canadians to be a voice opposing human trafficking, defending parental rights, lowering taxes, affirming the dignity of all human life, combating anti-Semitism, protecting charitable status for faith-based organizations, and protecting women from violence. She regularly appears on national media platforms and has led hundreds of young Canadians on leadership delegations to Parliament to meet with Members of Parliament and Senators. She is widely respected as one of Canada's leading voices in grassroots civic engagement, particularly in the faith community.

Faytene is happily married to Robert, and together they have two children.

Manufactured by Amazon.ca
Acheson, AB

32841680R00107